"This is a beautiful and original book in which Anthony Ward shares with us a life shaped by his love of flowers. And through vivid prose and stunning photographs, [he] brings into the living room the magic of these gifts from the world of nature."

—JANE GOODALL, DBE, FOUNDER, THE JANE GOODALL INSTITUTE

"Tears came to my eyes many times as I read this wise, soulful, and loving book. Anthony Ward, who is himself as mysterious as a flower, has written beautifully about his relationship with flowers. Not perhaps since George Washington Carver have we had the opportunity to learn from so evolved a mystic soul about the possibility of human interaction with, and appreciation of, plants.

"This is one of those books that make us say: This book, these teachings, this calm spirit, have been missing from my life! And, thanks to so good a universe as the one we share, now it exists!"

—ALICE WALKER, POET, ACTIVIST, PULITZER PRIZE-WINNING AUTHOR

"One can always identify Anthony's work, which he receives directly from the Creator. The work is organic, pure, and innocent. I'm so happy that Anthony has finally put into form this much dreamt about and visioned book that you will be blessed to hold in your hands. Anthony himself is a flower."

—GURMUKH KHALSA, FOUNDER, GOLDEN BRIDGE YOGA CENTER, LOS ANGELES, PIONEER IN THE FIELD OF PRENATAL YOGA

"*Being with Flowers* offers a performative meditation that encourages our contemplation of sublime beauty, drawing together heaven and earth to grace mind and soul. To watch Anthony perform with flowers is like seeing a magician sculpt plant life into its most radiant beauty. Creating exquisite floral art for the Dalai Lama, Hollywood's elite, and performing onstage with jam bands and electronic musicians, Anthony charms the audience while ceremonially showing us what we miss when we pass a grassy grove without thorough examination. He reminds us we are all 'being with flowers' and encourages us to embrace our tree-hugging love of the environment with a sacred bouquet."

—ALLYSON AND ALEX GREY, VISIONARY ARTISTS, AUTHORS, AND COFOUNDERS, THE CHAPEL OF SACRED MIRRORS, NEW YORK

"I have been blessed to witness the magic that is Anthony being with flowers. People all over the world will now have the chance to experience his sacred, beautiful, and empowering process through his book. His experiences with flowers have beautiful and inspiring lessons for living life for all of us."

—JULIA BUTTERFLY HILL, AUTHOR, *THE LEGACY OF LUNA*, AND COFOUNDER, THE CIRCLE OF LIFE FOUNDATION

being with
FLOWERS

FLORAL ART AS SPIRITUAL PRACTICE

ANTHONY WARD

VISIONARY FLORAL SCULPTOR

QUARRY

Quarto is the authority on a wide range of topics.

Quarto educates, entertains and enriches the lives of our readers—enthusiasts and lovers of hands-on living.

www.QuartoKnows.com

First published in the United States of America in 2017 by Quarry Books, an imprint of Quarto Publishing Group USA Inc.
100 Cummings Center
Suite 265-D
Beverly, Massachusetts 01915-6101
Telephone: (978) 282-9590
Fax: (978) 283-2742
QuartoKnows.com
Visit our blogs at QuartoKnows.com

10 9 8 7 6 5 4 3 2 1

ISBN: 978-1-63159-135-8
Digital edition published in 2017.

Library of Congress Cataloging-in-Publication Data
Names: Ward, Anthony (Flower arranger)
Title: Being with flowers : floral art as spiritual practice : meditations on
    conscious flower arranging to inspire peace, beauty, and the everyday
    sacred / Anthony Ward.
Description: Beverly, Massachusetts : Quarry Books, [2017] | Includes index.
Identifiers: LCCN 2016034396 | ISBN 9781631591358 (hardback)
Subjects: LCSH: Flower arrangement. | Meditation.
Classification: LCC SB449 .W2975 2017 | DDC 635.9/66--dc23
LC record available at https://lccn.loc.gov/2016034396

Design and Page Layout: Sandra Salamony
Cover Image: Shutterstock
Photography: All photography by John Felix Shaw, except page 16, LeAnna Cargman; page 23, Anthony Ward; page 62, Molly Harrell; pages 96 and 115, Jeff Marsh; page 155, Lucas Samaras.
Illustration: Shutterstock, Sandra Salamony

Printed in China

MIX
Paper from responsible sources
FSC® C016973

For my ancestors, and also my mother
Zelma Darling White Ward and father
Oscar Melvin Ward, who gave me life so that
I could journey with the FLOWERS:

*"Fantastic Love Offerings Welcoming
Everyone Revealing Souls."*

Contents

INTRODUCTION

My Communion with Nature

LIKE MANY OF THE teachers in my life, Sojourner Troussant is a woman. Her clear, smooth skin is blue-black, with the keen and stunning features of those African masks from the Ivory Coast. We first crossed paths at the Inner City Cultural Center of Los Angeles, where I had a dance scholarship in ballet. I was nineteen years old. Standing before our class, her eyes were clear as she spoke with purpose in every syllable: "You've got to prepare. You've got to trim away the excess. In a sense, that's what 'prepare' means!" As she spoke, she mimed trimming an apple. "If you want to be a dancer, you must BE dance." This is one lesson I take with me as my journey with the flowers continues. I sometimes still hear her voice as I do my work.

I elected to take a dance scholarship instead of attend college, so my formal "book-learned" education ended after high school. Most of my public education is a dull memory, but one year stands out as clear as if it happened last week: seventh grade. It was a revolutionary year in my life. I had just turned thirteen—finally, a teenager. That was the year I discovered sex in my body. It was the year I really started to listen to music and began to fantasize about being a dancer. Thankfully it was Stevie Wonder, Joni Mitchell, Sarah Vaughan, and an eclectic, illustrious mesh of

music that wafted through our home. It was also the year that I was introduced to the work of Maya Angelou through a teacher's reading of *I Know Why the Caged Bird Sings*.

I'd known for a while that I was different from the other boys, and it had always made me feel very alone, but that was the year that my family suddenly became aware of that difference. Even my mother, who I knew loved me deeply, was all of a sudden seemingly unable to accept me as I was. *I Know Why the Caged Bird Sings* was a life raft for me during that difficult time. Maya Angelou's head-on grappling with the human condition helped me realize that I'd be okay. Because she had the courage to come out and share her horrible experiences the way she did, I knew I would somehow find my way.

A REVELATION

At that time in my life we lived in a neighborhood with a lake. One day I went down to the lake, as I often did, just to be alone and sit by the water. I remember being overwhelmed with the feeling that perhaps my family would be better off without me. For some reason, on this particular day I looked down into the water. I saw my face and behind that I saw the clouds, and all at once there was blur and I knew—the water,

my face, the clouds—that I was a part of this picture, this ancient and huge picture. It had nothing to do with my family, or the kids at school. It was way bigger than that and I was a part of it.

I was part of the sky; I was part of the water. I belonged to something that was made by the Creator of all. I knew in that moment that I need give no excuse. I need not even talk—I could just BE. I was enough, and whole, and I belonged to this Earth just as I was. I knew in that instant that my communion with nature was deep, profound, simple, and abiding, and that somehow this realization would carry me into the mystery that was to come. As I stood up, a blossom fell in the lake and created a seemingly infinite, concentric circle. I knew I was home, within myself.

I know my communion with nature began within the heartbeats of my ancestors, but in my life, my deep

connection began that year I turned thirteen. Mother Earth had beckoned me to plant radish seeds in her womb, in a secret garden I'd created behind the shed in our backyard. Six weeks later I had full-grown radishes—just like the package said. I ran down the hillside of our sprawling middle-class backyard in Fayetteville, North Carolina, incredibly excited to show the ripe bounty to my mother and my grandmother. My father's mother, Dollie Mae Hall—or Mother Mae, as we called her—was visiting us because my eldest sister Ann was getting married. Mother Mae made a fuss about how proud she was of me for growing food that I could share with my family. She herself was an avid gardener and yearly won her neighborhood's Nicest Garden award. My mother made me feel proud by asking me to bless the food that evening. *God is great and God is good, and we thank Him for our food. Amen. God is love.*

THE MENTOR'S GIFT

My respect for nature may have begun in the garden, but my professional career with flowers began when I became an apprentice to Wilbur G. Davis Jr. at My Son the Florist in Los Angeles in 1993. Wilbur was a young, articulate, college-educated black man with a degree in biology. His family was from New Orleans, and they were descendants of some of the first slaves in that area. Wilbur accomplished a lot in a short time. In ten years, he went from doing his work in his apartment to being offered $1.5 million for his thriving floral business. His clientele was a virtual who's who of Hollywood, with regular orders from the likes of Elizabeth Taylor, the Gettys, Cindra Ladd, Sally Field, Tim Burton, Geena Davis, the Los Angeles County

Museum of Art, and the Los Angeles Philharmonic. If you were in Los Angeles in those days and you knew flowers, you knew who Wilbur was.

Although I had no experience with floral arranging, Wilbur hired me over other trained designers because of how impressed he was with some calla lilies I had grown, which I donated to him for the arrangements he was working on for my friend's wedding. He could tell from looking at those lilies just how much I loved flowers. He would say, "I could teach you how to prepare the flowers and the mechanics of arranging them, but I could never give you what you already have, which is an obvious and deep love for flowers." When he fell ill with AIDS, he said he needed my energy and enthusiasm around. Learning my craft from a master floral artist who knew his days were numbered was an amazing blessing. He created every piece as though it may be his last. I stayed with Wilbur for about a year, until we felt I was ready to move on.

SHARING THE GIFT

I left Los Angeles and moved to Santa Cruz, California, in 1994. After six months there, I opened my own shop called Passionflora Floral Art. The community of Santa Cruz embraced my work and within a year I was the most

sought-after floral designer there. I had a custom studio and saw clients by appointment only. This allowed me to work with a more affluent clientele and gave me time to enjoy the beauty that is so overwhelming in an ocean town filled with redwood trees.

In my current business, Being with Flowers, I have been hired to create for people whose names are well known, as well as for names you certainly would not recognize. For me, the work itself is the reason I do it. And that is enough. My communion with nature sometimes deafens me to all else. There is no sound except the rustling of flower petals, the slice of my paring knife, the snip of my clippers. Being with Flowers is a manifestation of that communion. I know Mother Nature is the greatest artist of all, and, at my best, I am only a vessel of the vibration that keeps nature flourishing. My work is a soul-level connection with that vibration. To me each flower is a masterpiece. Flowers disarm us; they are one of the greatest gifts that we can give.

I aspire to share my work with as many of my brothers and sisters in the family of humankind as possible. When people tell me that because of my work, they take walks and notice things they have never noticed before, it is the greatest compliment that I could receive. If my communion with nature can help people marvel as I do at the abundance we are given from Mother Earth, then I am deeply blessed. The first blessing is my own communion with nature, which is a very private thing. The second blessing is sharing that with others.

This is my journey. My goal for this book is to inspire you to go deeper within your own journey with the flowers.

With Passion, Love, and Light,

Anthony

1

The Garden We Call Earth

Earth is an abundant garden, thriving and somehow unstoppable. Though not always tended in a mindful manner, our garden still flourishes; it is our home. My spiritual awakenings often happen in the garden. Many times I choose to experience nature alone, in silence. Without the distraction of words, complete attention can be given to the natural world. When did you last take a walk outside, by yourself, in silence? If you have not done this, I suggest you do it soon. Our planet's landscape changes rapidly, and we should not take for granted what is here now. Even if you live in a city, it is possible to find natural spaces to get lost in.

I aspire to help you go deeper into your own journey with the flowers, which will require diligent work on your part. Be aware of the flowers in your life. What flowers are growing in your yard, your neighbor's yard, your city block? Spend time at your local flower shop. Allow the beauty of flowers to enter your daily consciousness. To do this is quite simple: notice them.

MEDITATION:
Single Flower

BRINGING EASY, peaceful feelings into your life will be a gift to both you and the world around you. Meditating on a single flower can help you do this. Make time in your life to give yourself this precious gift. The best time for this meditation is whenever you can find fifteen minutes to be alone. Waking up before others in your home is an ideal way to start your day.

This Single Flower meditation was inspired by the words of that wonderful painter of flowers, Georgia O'Keeffe, who is famously known to have said, "If you take a flower in your hand and really look at it, it's your world for the moment."

In the spirit of that quotation, please choose one single bloom and, while sitting comfortably and in silence, hold that flower gently in your hands. Look deeply at what you are holding. The flower is there for you to fully enjoy. Smell it. Stroke the petals. Just *be* with the flower. The contemplation of this

beauty will help you go deeper into the heart space of your own humanity. Behold the flower's sacred invitation into what visionary artist Alex Grey calls "the momentary face of God."

KOKORO NO HANA

The Japanese have a phrase for the invitation the flowers and I extend to you. *Kokoro no hana*, or "heart of the flower." This is the path of flower study, flower meditation, flower *power*. It is a path that will bring much beauty and joy to your life. If you want a more beautiful life, notice the flowers as you pass them. Literally stop and smell the roses.

Your Relationship with Flowers

ECKHART TOLLE, in his revolutionary book *A New Earth*, said, "As the consciousness of human beings developed, flowers were most likely the first thing they came to value that had no utilitarian purpose for them." To fully understand this vital, ancient, and very pivotal relationship we have with flowers, let us imagine that it never happened. Where would we humans be in our evolutionary trajectory without flowers? Where would we be without flowers in our everyday lives?

I want you to imagine a world without flowers. I mean close your eyes and really picture it. Imagine a spring without flowers. Now imagine a wedding, a funeral, the grocery store, or a botanical garden without flowers. This is almost impossible to picture because we have become so very accustomed to seeing flowers in these settings. As my friend

Gurmukh Kaur Khalsa, whom *Vanity Fair* magazine calls "the Goddess of Kundalini Yoga," says, "I can't imagine a world without flowers. It would be like not having water."

"There are always flowers for those who want to see them."

—HENRI MATISSE

PLAYING FAVORITES

Flowers can certainly brighten a room or bring life to a forgotten corner in your home. But how often do you deeply see a flower? Do you have a favorite flower? I am often asked this. The real answer is this: whatever flower I happen to be holding at the moment. I truly love all flowers equally, just as flowers love all of us equally. If a daffodil were sitting in front of someone you thought of as abhorrent, that flower would give off its radiance, fragrance, and visual beauty for that person just as much as it would for someone you admire. There is a true equanimity in the offering of love that comes from flowers.

Our lives often unfold as a series of relationships. From birth to death, we breathe and engage in relationships that shape our perceptions, personality, and experiences. I learned to love flowers from watching my mother, Zelma Darling White Ward, love her children. Sometimes, when my mother looked

at me, I felt as if the sun was rising on my face. The amazing thing was, every single one of her eight children felt the same way.

We were eight very different personalities, each one encouraged to think and speak for him- and herself. We all had our own way of seeking attention from the family. Some of us were well behaved, some could be mischievous, but our mother had a way of making us all feel as if we were the special one. In much the same way, every time I hold a flower, that flower is, for me, the special one.

GRANDMOTHER MUH

Flowers have played an important role in my life from a very early age. I was born in San Antonio, Texas, yet I spent the first eight years of my life growing up on air force bases in France and Germany. My father had served in World War II, and after risking his life for his country, he was disheartened by the racism he encountered living in the South after the war. He asked to be transferred back to Europe, as he and my mother wanted their eight children to see themselves, and be seen, in a different way than the United States allowed for at that time. This was a visionary decision and one for which I am still so very grateful.

Because we attended American schools on the bases, we did not learn the languages while we lived there, but we were afforded rich cultural experiences that growing up in San Antonio would not have allowed. We must have been quite a sight at the Oktoberfest in Germany—four little black boys in lederhosen with our four sisters in traditional German dirndl dresses. I think Mom and Dad must have had an ironic sense of humor as we partook in these types of experiences.

When my family returned to the United States, we visited our grandmothers and other relatives in San Antonio. We would all congregate at the home of my mother's parents, Alvis and Luvie White. Luvie was the matriarch of our large family. We called her Muh. She was the daughter of Mary Magdalene Henderson, a woman who was very knowledgeable about herbs. Muh was also an avid gardener. It was

"Give me odorous at sunrise a garden of beautiful flowers where I can walk undisturbed."

—WALT WHITMAN

a rite of passage for us grandchildren to jump off Muh's porch without getting into one of her abundant flowerbeds. There were thirty of us grandchildren, and none of us ever fell in. You simply did not even try unless you knew you were up to it, as the famed "switch" tree was just around the corner.

Muh was sometimes terrifying to me, although it was always apparent how much she loved us. She was very gruff, often yelling and ordering someone around. She had a raspy voice that was seldom quiet.

One morning, I noticed a woman out in the garden. I remember being confused because it looked like Muh, but her expression was so very different than the scowl I was used to seeing. She had a calm smile on her face, and there were butterflies flying around her almost like they wanted to land. She was watering her garden with a wand, and the plants—a wide array of hostas and brightly colored zinnias in the sunnier areas—seemed to lean into her as she passed.

Who is this sweet lady? I thought. I went outside and quietly followed her around. I was especially astounded

WISDOM FROM ALICE

I once related my story about Muh to writer and activist Alice Walker. Her insight was that my grandmother felt safe in her garden. I wish I could follow Alice around with a tape recorder. She always gets right to the truth of the matter and relates it in the most unassuming way.

when she saw me and smiled as a butterfly landed on her shoulder. Watching my often-scary grandmother transform into this goddess in her garden caused me to look at what it was she was doing that had created such a difference in her demeanor. It was in that moment that I first really noticed the flowers. They seemed, to my eight-year-old, very imaginative eyes, to literally be smiling at her as she passed.

THE IMPORTANCE OF WORDS

To deepen our relationship with flowers, we must change the language with which we speak of them. When I first began my career in floral design, I was an apprentice at My Son the Florist in Los Angeles in the 1990s. My job was to prepare the flowers for the designers and clean up after them when they were finished. I would often hear them say, "Let's use roses in that arrangement," or "Let's use orchids in that centerpiece," and so on. The word *use* never sat well with me, and I decided early on that when I opened my own establishment, I would say, "Let's *work with* roses in that arrangement" and "Let's *work with* orchids in that centerpiece." We establish relationships with our words. So let's *work with* flowers, not *use* them.

The first time I taught my workshop, "Being with Flowers: Floral Art as Spiritual Practice," I had a student who had been a florist for many years. She told me that she felt like she had an entirely new job because she had made that simple change in her vocabulary. If you don't like the word *work*, how about *play*? Find a word that is comfortable for you—anything but *use*. It is the intention behind the things we do that really makes the difference, so let's start with the intention to *co-create* with the flowers.

Flowers for Yourself

IN WINTER, when my own garden is not abundant with flowers, local stores are my go-to source. The mixed bouquet I worked with here had three white roses, three white spider mums, three white alstroemeria, one stem of white oriental lily, one stem of blue statice, three stems of blue thistle, and three stems of white stock. Every time you buy a mixed bouquet, the flowers may be different. Allow the stems and arches of the flowers to guide you, always keeping in mind the way the flowers grow in their natural setting.

Gathering greenery or branches is an ideal way to bring the beauty of nature into your home. Always ask permission from any property owner before gathering. Here I added a flowering plum branch from my neighbor's yard. She was more than happy to share her abundance for this creation.

Fill the vessel with water, almost to the top. Take a moment to acknowledge the blessing of this water. Submerge the branches or vines to create a snug fit.

Remove plastic from the store-bought flowers. Separate the greenery from the flowers and place the greenery inside around the mouth of the vessel. The goal is to hide the rim of the vessel.

I find it most desirable to work with odd numbers when creating any arrangement. Think of the vessel separated in that way as well. This arrangement was created to live against a wall. To create for this setting, it is important to keep in mind the three-quarters of the vessel that will be viewed, but remember that there should be movement in the back of the vessel as well, just enough so that the back of the arrangement does not appear flat.

Now is the time to make a flower offering for you. Before you begin, take

MATERIALS

Glass vessel

Curly willow or grape vine branches

One large bunch of mixed flowers

a moment to feel the air moving in and out of your body. Acknowledge that you are alive and well enough to have the luxury to create.

Incorporate spider mums into greenery around mouth of vessel and then add roses and oriental lily in the upper central area of arrangement. Their stems call for this prominent position.

Add remaining flowers in a way that complements and interplays with the flowers you have already placed. Add one white flowering plum branch to enliven the piece.

Floral Sculpture in the Garden

CHOOSE AN empty space for your creation. If possible, find a place that you can tend and change throughout the year. I've found a spot near a wall that is partially shaded by a covered deck, but this can also be done in a window box. The idea is to create a garden that appears to be growing where once there was nothing.

Take a moment and sit in silence near the area in which you are about to create. Open yourself to the possibilities of how the flowers and you will work together to transform the space.

The area in which you will create can be as simple as a bed of moss or rocks. Perhaps add a favorite statue, sculpture, interesting tree stump, or special crystals.

Different-sized water tubes with pointy tips will be invaluable as your creation unfolds. Place fresh-cut flowers into the tubes and then insert the tubes into premoistened soil or moss.

SEASONAL CHANGES

These offerings were created in the same area at different times of the year. They help illustrate how this space can be seasonally transformed. This space can be a focal point in your garden and a way to deepen your connection with the earth.

MATERIALS

Moss, sod, or pebbles for ground cover

Jumbo aqua picks or water tubes

Single-stem blooms (mums, roses, and daffodils work well)

Potted plants, such as ivy or succulents (optional)

The Buddha sculpture is a focal point, so flowers are placed accordingly. Mirror the way flowers grow in their natural setting. This will guide you toward a more harmonious offering.

Flowers drink water at variable rates. Lift one flower of each type at the end of twenty-four hours to see how fast your flowers are drinking. Refill the water tubes accordingly.

2

Floral Art as Spiritual Practice

Our lives are as sacred as we choose. A walk in the park can be a meditation. When I gather a branch from a tree, I bow to that tree. When I take a flower from a plant, I say "thank you" to the plant. Meaning: "Deep thanks to this amazing blue planet that offers up such sweetness." Long ago, when I realized this work is the reason I was incarnated, I made a promise that I would do it for the higher good.

I once had the honor of creating a flower offering for a lecture given by the dearly departed Lama Tharchin Rinpoche, a high lama in the Tibetan Buddhist tradition. His lecture was about sacred art, and he opened by stating that the person who had created the arrangement on stage had created sacred art, by giving the flowers a new home. It is our responsibility to care for the flowers. The arrangements we create will lovingly give them a new home. Time flies. We are only guaranteed this breath, this moment. Allow the flowers to make your life more sacred.

MEDITATION:

Walking Flower

ZEN MASTER Thich Nhat Hanh has so much to teach us. He is the inspiration for the Walking Flower meditation.

Begin by standing comfortably in a natural setting where you feel safe, such as a park, your yard, or a rural area with little traffic. Take a moment to focus on your breathing. Breathe in and out at a slow, measured pace at least ten times. Start walking, and lead with your heel in a heel-ball-toe fashion. The steps you take should be very slow and exaggerated. You are not walking toward anything specific, but simply taking conscious steps, aware of your feet on the earth and the air moving in and out of your lungs. The purpose of this meditation is to bring you to the present moment, and to help you relate to the earth in a peaceful, mindful manner. This exercise should be done for at least ten minutes or longer.

It is important to open our eyes to the beauty that flowers offer us. Of the many blessings in life that this garden we call Earth gives us, flowers are our garden's glory. One of my students said

it very well: "Flowers were put here simply to delight us." A botanist or a scientist might disagree, but at the heart of the matter, my student revealed the essential truth of how flowers touch us.

PEACEFUL STEPS

Zen Master Thich Nhat Hanh teaches us about walking meditations in *Peace Is Every Step: The Path of Mindfulness in Everyday Life*. He instructs us to "be aware of the contact between your feet and the earth. Walk as if you are kissing the earth with your feet."

He goes on to say, "We have caused a lot of damage to the earth. Now is the time for us to take good care of her. We bring our peace and calm to the surface of the earth and share the lesson of love. We walk in that spirit."

"From time to time when we see something beautiful, we may want to stop and look at it—a tree, a flower, some children playing. As we look, we continue to follow our breathing, lest we lose the beautiful flower and get caught up in our thoughts. When we want to resume walking, we just start again. Each step we take will create a cool breeze, refreshing our body and mind. Every step makes a flower bloom under our feet. We can do it only if we do not think of the future or the past, if we know that life can be found in the present moment."

—THICH NHAT HANH, *PEACE IS EVERY STEP: THE PATH OF MINDFULNESS IN EVERYDAY LIFE*

Flowers as Our Teachers

ALTHOUGH I MAY NOT have a favorite flower, certain flowers have played a pivotal role in my own life's journey. These particular flowers keep showing up and teaching me valuable lessons that I carry with me, lessons that I didn't see coming. For this reason, there are certain flowers that I consider special teachers.

SUNFLOWERS

Sunflowers have always been one of these flowers. The first year I began working with flowers professionally, I created a small garden in the tiny yard of the garage/coach house in Los Angeles that I occupied at the time. I had several very tall sunflowers at the back of the garden—one was almost 14 ft (4 m) tall. There was a little girl living next door who would always come over and watch me while I worked. One day I heard her say to her mother, "Mommy, I am going out to watch The Flower Man water his flowers."

That was the first time anyone had called me The Flower Man. Years later when I moved to Santa Cruz, California, it would be the name by which many people in that town called me. It is also what my dear friend, the beloved singer/songwriter Michael Franti, calls me and how he introduces me when I create arrangements live on stage with his band.

Sunflowers are a favorite flower for many people. Right now, in my garden, I have more than a hundred planted. They are a wonderful flower to plant with children, because of how quickly they grow. The stalk rises seemingly before their eyes, and before they know it, the sunflower is taller than they are, which always fascinates them.

SUNFLOWER FACE MANDALA

When sunflower petals begin to fall out, a wonderful way of celebrating the sunflower for its "last hurrah" is to take the loose petals and place them around a picture of the face of someone you love. I like to do this as a meditation, placing each petal with a blessing for the joy, prosperity, and good health of my loved one. The face in this sunflower belongs to my friend, healer Ditlev Dharmakaya.

THE STRENGTH OF SIMPLICITY

To me, in this art form, I feel as though I am working with masterpieces when I arrange flowers—each individual flower is already a masterpiece. The first time I was to create a flower offering for Thich Nhat Hanh, I received a valuable lesson from sunflowers. The event was in Oakland, California, and was to begin at 7 p.m. Well, at 7 p.m., I was on the Bay Bridge, stuck in traffic. I was so stressed out and concerned about my career. I remember thinking, *Nobody will take me seriously again, I am so late.*

I began to breathe slowly, as Thay—which means "teacher" in Vietnamese and is what his students call him—himself suggests in these stressful times. At that moment, I looked over and saw a miraculous sunset. I thought to myself, *What would Thich Nhat Hanh do?* Answer: Enjoy the sunset. I certainly did, and I arrived an hour late.

His students were so very kind. They offered me tea and showed me to a seat they had saved for me. I sat down, and as I looked up at the altar from which Thich Nhat Hanh spoke, I was taken aback by the arrangement some friends of mine had made in my absence. It was a tall, stout arrangement of about eleven fully opened sunflowers. For this man, it was just right. In my van, I had vines and branches and many types of flowers for the arrangement I was going to create, but the sight of that simple arrangement was so very humbling.

The lesson I learned that evening was crucial: if one is making an arrangement for someone else, make it for *them*, for the spirit in which they present themselves. The point is not to try to impress them or anyone else. I was certainly out to impress that night with all that I had brought, but those simply arranged sunflowers were the perfect embodiment of Thich Nhat Hanh's mindful wisdom.

REFLECTING PEACE

The first event where I created an altar for His Holiness the Dalai Lama, I was given the precious gift of a few moments alone with him. The producer of the event, Tibet House, is headed by Robert and Nena Thurman. They arranged a brief meeting between His Holiness and me as a gesture of thanks for all of the work that my staff and I had done for this illustrious event, which was a conference in San Francisco called "Peacemaking: The Power of Nonviolence." This event was created to help inner-city youths deal with violent situations in nonviolent ways.

That day I had decided that when I met him, I was going to hand him a sunflower. Our meeting was scheduled for three o'clock. At noon, I spotted the sunflower that I wanted to present to him, and I carried it around with me until the time came. I remember he exited his town car with a swarm of bodyguards, walked right up to me, and Robert introduced us.

At that point, I handed him the sunflower, and His Holiness let out a joyful sigh. He held the sunflower in one hand, and with his other hand, he reached out and grabbed both of my hands, which were in prayer position. He began massaging my hands as he spoke words of such loving kindness.

In that moment, I realized what being in the presence of a truly evolved human being feels like. He is human, yet he prepares himself every day at 4 a.m. to be the most loving individual he can be that day. I have witnessed this many times since, as I have had the honor of creating for him in this way many times since 1996. Whenever I create for the Dalai Lama, the sunflower is always a focal point for these arrangements.

OPPORTUNITIES FOR BEAUTY

"When he creates floral offerings for the Dalai Lama, Anthony Ward loves to include sunflowers—'for his smile,' says Ward, 'and the color of his robes.'

"The way Ward works with sunflowers is a lesson in how many ways there are to look at the same plant. When he's putting several sunflowers in a large arrangement, he likes to place the first one as if it is saying hello. Sunflowers can do that. He might pull some yellow petals from a flower and strew them across other objects on the table, or rub the pollen-covered stamen away from the flower head, revealing a mandala of seeds that you can set on the table as a centerpiece or hang on the wall to contemplate. And why not float the flower heads in the lily pond?

"When others might toss faded blooms in the compost, Ward sees more opportunities for beauty. Among his containers of fresh flowers, there might be a bucket with a dozen sunflower heads floating upside down, hydrating before being placed on the altar at the foot of some new bouquet. For a few days the flowers will look fairly fresh, even out of the water, and then begin to dry. Some flowers dry exquisitely, fading and shrinking into skeletons of their former selves, revealing how much there is to see beneath the surface."

—RONNIE SHUSHAN,
EXCERPT FROM *SPIRITUALITY & HEALTH*, 2006

ROSES

Roses are valuable teachers. Their stems have thorns, as a reminder to us to always stay in the moment when we are working with them. When I was in high school, one of my chores was to mow the lawn and take care of the garden. My mother had a rose garden that rested beneath a giant sugar maple tree. I had read up on the proper way to maintain roses, and was very diligent in doing so.

However, one day when I was not paying attention to what I was doing, I reached down to pick up my clippers, and my forearm collided with a robust, thorny stem. Three large thorns dug into my arm. I immediately pulled back, and one of the thorns broke off, lodged in my skin. The pain was so excruciating, I almost passed out. I carry this lesson with me to this day when I am working with roses. Roses are an important metaphor for life: that sometimes beauty and pain can be intrinsically linked.

Are there any flowers that trigger an emotional response in you, either positive or negative? I once met a woman who told me she could not stand to be around tulips. She never knew why until her mother passed away. She was going through her mother's old photos, and in one photo there she was, all of six years old and with a grimace on her face, surrounded by tulips. She told me she remembers that everyone kept saying, "Smile for the camera." Well, earlier that day she had been told that her father would no longer be living with them. She was a real daddy's girl and was devastated by that news. Of course she had trouble smiling for the camera. She spent most of her life absolutely detesting tulips and never knew why, until she saw that photo.

"It's been proven by quite a few studies that plants are good for our psychological development. If you green an area, the rate of crime goes down. Torture victims begin to recover when they spend time outside in a garden with flowers. So we need them, in some deep psychological sense, which I don't suppose anybody really understands yet."

—JANE GOODALL,
SMITHSONIAN MAGAZINE, 2013

BEAUTY IS IN THE EYE OF THE BEHOLDER

We humans have a tendency to place our egos on everything we do. Some flowers are considered, in our collective consciousness, to be dowdy, while others are considered elegant, but that says more about humans than it does about the flowers themselves. Some people absolutely loathe hydrangeas. Carnations and baby's breath are often singled out as "undesirable," while orchids are held in high regard. I sometimes like to pair orchids with native grasses, which many people consider to be weeds, because I believe they make a stunning combination.

One warm summer night in Los Angeles, I was enjoying the garden that I had spent the day caring for. It was a full moon, and the air was heavy with the sweet smell of *Stephanotis floribunda*. A robust vine—glistening with white clusters of the trumpet-shaped flowers—reached all the way from the ground up into the telephone wires high above. This was a private garden, densely camouflaged and out of view from anyone else's eyes. Above my head was a hanging basket that was lush with flowering sky-blue lobelia and succulents. The beauty of this sight struck me deeply, and I was so taken

aback that I started to say "oh my God," but what came out of my mouth was "I am God."

All at once, my entire body felt like it had an internal earthquake—from the bottom of my spine through the roof of my head, there was a heat and pulse extending seemingly into the heavens. I had an awareness of my body from outside of it. This coursing power was so immense that I felt as though I could float if I were only able to control it. It was so intense that all I could do was just go with it. My eyes were transfixed on the full moon, yet I was aware of objects outside of this view, of the flowers around me. I stayed this way for what seemed an eternity. When the energy broke, I fell to the ground and began weeping uncontrollably. I could not walk, so I crawled into my home. I

"Weeds are flowers, too, once you get to know them."

—A. A. MILNE

immediately looked at the clock, which hung by the door, and realized this had all happened in less than ten minutes.

When I could speak without crying, I called a wise woman I had befriended and with whom I had recently done some energy work called pulsing. She listened to my story intently, and when I was done she said, "This is your experience. You don't have to call it anything, but just know, what happened to you is something people spend lifetimes doing yoga, meditating, and experimenting with psychoactive drugs in order to experience. This rich experience will be yours forever and you will encounter it again." I was so very grateful that she had been there to talk to after it happened.

To be clear, this profound experience was not one that induced me to feel that I *am* God, but rather opened my heart and my eyes wider to the under-standing that the Creator of all wonders lives in *all* things—the flowers, the trees, each and every one of us.

Do you have a special connection with any particular flowers? Sunflowers, roses, tulips? How have they shaped, and in some instances perhaps guided, your life? As beloved singer-songwriter Ani DiFranco says, "God's work isn't done by God; it's done by people." When I am working at my best, this is what I am doing. To get in touch with the divine spark that you are, recognize that connection to creation that lives and breathes in you. It is available to you at all times.

Create a Personal Altar

FOR THOUSANDS of years, flowers have played an integral role in many spiritual and religious rituals. Certainly, altar creation is one such practice.

Is there a place in your home that you would call an altar? Spiritual teacher Ram Dass reminds us that an altar is a place to keep pictures and remembrances of those we cherish in a sacred way. Bringing flowers to such places helps set the sacred tone that will elevate both this altar and your life in general. What makes an altar significant for you? To me, anywhere we place a flower with intention becomes an altar. Creating an altar in your home can be a way to bring the sacred into your everyday life.

Select a space to create your altar. I prefer a low table so that I can kneel before it, but side tables, accent tables, benches—anything works. Perhaps even set aside a corner of your desk or kitchen table. The size and location matter less than the intention behind the creation. The table can be covered with a tablecloth or runner, but this is not necessary. Sometimes the beauty of simple wood can be breathtaking by itself.

Set your intention and clearly decide what the purpose of this altar will be. Is it a devotion to a loved one? A call for abundance? A place where you remind yourself to live in gratitude? Spend time gathering any photos, mementos, or special personal items that you wish to be inside the energy of the sacred space you are creating.

Arrange the items in a manner befitting your intention. The flowers placed here should reflect what this personal altar represents for you. Perhaps they are the favorite flowers of those whom you wish to honor. I like to create around one focal flower and place the rest of the flowers low around the table. Place any candles last. Light your candles with prayerful intention—and don't forget to blow them out when you are finished!

thought

A single flower, placed with intention and love, creates an altar.

ALTAR FOR THE LIVING MUSE

The muse for this slightly futuristic flower offering is a stylish, avant-garde performance artist and social activist with a penchant for theatrical attire who shines her light on all around her. Flowers are there to shine their light on all who come before them. With this open and really divine love, call yourself to the moment by gently rubbing your hands together. Cherish your hands. They will perform the good work you will do with the flowers. As always before you begin, take time to simply breathe. Acknowledge the moment you have been given.

muse

A person, or a force personified as a person, who is the source of inspiration for a creative artist. (With passion for Gaga.)

Secure the disco balls to the vessel housing with raffia. The majority of the disco balls should be placed above the top lip of the vessel, if possible.	Fill the glass vessel with water and place it inside of the vessel housing. Wind curly willow branches down into the vessel. Allow the ends to rise out of the vessel above the disco balls.	Place the berry clusters, around the mouth of the vessel. Loop the bear grass in concentric circles around the berries at varying levels.

MATERIALS

Miniature disco balls

Wrought-iron stand or other unique
additional housing for vessel

Raffia or twine

Glass vessel

Curly willow branches

Berry clusters

Bear grass

Cymbidium orchid spray

Scotch broom

Place the orchids in the center of the vessel.
Frame them with additional curly willow
and a few stalks of Scotch broom to fully
enhance their glory.

Place the arrangement on an altar table.
Incorporate items that exemplify the feelings evoked by your personal muse. Single
blooms in mosaic vases capture the spirit of
this particular muse.

Altars for the Public Space

IN CREATING ALTARS, I found a deeper meaning in the work that I do. I have been honored to create altar spaces not only for His Holiness the Dalai Lama, Ram Dass, and Thich Nhat Hanh, but also for Alice Walker, Deepak Chopra, and many others whose work has touched my life in significant ways, including Maya Angelou. To be able to offer my work to her and develop a personal relationship with her were incredible blessings, because she was such an important influence in my life.

I had the honor of creating for Maya Angelou many times during her illustrious life. On these auspicious occasions, I often created a "caged bird," with birds of paradise singing for her. Once we had more than three hundred on one stage with her. The backdrop was made up of 12 ft (3.6 m)-tall flowering apple branches. I'll never forget when she said, "Look at what Anthony has done with these flowers on stage. I have never been surrounded by more beauty in my entire life." I sat weeping in the front row.

It was Maya Angelou who gave me the title of "floral sculptor." Backstage at one event, as we stood in the wings, she looked out onto the stage at my creations and said to me, "Anthony, this is big art. *Big art*. You are not a 'florist.' You are a 'floral sculptor.'" When I am asked what I call myself, I now respond with "floral sculptor," with gratitude to her.

When creating a space for His Holiness the Dalai Lama at a ceremonial event, I am often given free rein to create pieces to frame his throne chair. Sometimes, though, his personal aides advise me of what flowers are most appropriate for a location nearest him. Which reminds me: always make sure that the people you are creating for do not have any allergies. The idea behind honoring this person starts with your awareness of such things.

Several times, I have created offerings to adorn the stage at Carnegie Hall, most often for the amazing pianist Katya Grineva. I created one piece to sit within the curve of her Steinway

A caged bird for Maya Angelou, with passion, from Anthony.

grand piano. To me, this was as spiritual an altar as any, because Katya plays with all her heart and soul. She has stunned audiences the world over and has played Carnegie Hall more than a dozen times.

When creating any altar, begin with your heart. This altar is your creation and may be placed where many people have the opportunity to allow it to lift their hearts. Consider both the size of the space and who will be viewing this altar. How else will the space be adorned? Are there additional

sculptures or other items? Placement of your creation should accent and adorn any other places of interest. Frame the lectern/pulpit or place the arrangement in a way that accents whatever will happen on the stage, as I did with the curve of the grand piano.

ADORNING DEITIES
AND THE BUDDHA

For millennia, flowers have played an integral part in spiritual practices. Much of this is in the adorning of altars. Oftentimes people place spiritual figures on these altars, which are representatives of the Divine, a manifestation in form of that which they hold sacred.

I experience great joy in adorning these sculptural representations. When creating these offerings, I find that really interacting with the sculptures is key in bringing their essence to life. I feel that placing flowers in strategic spots really helps achieve something special.

People often ask whether I am a Buddhist, and my answer is no, because I am available to all of the light, regardless of the tradition or philosophy behind it. However, many images of Buddha have been presented to me in my lifetime. For me, Buddha represents the fullness of life and offers a reminder that the present moment is really all we have.

I find such joy in adorning figures of Buddha. Desiring nothing, the Buddha gently smiles. It is my honor to place flowers at these embodiments of peace. It is my hope that those who look upon these offerings will be lifted higher into their humanity.

prayer

A silent prayer for public altars: "May all who look upon the
sight of these flowers be lifted into their hearts."

Ganesha, a Hindu deity with a human body and elephant head, is considered to be the remover of obstacles. He can be found at the entrance of many temples throughout India. He is also thought of as the patron of letters and learning. I have always found something so intrinsically wise and beautiful about elephants. During my trips to India, I was greeted with the image of Ganesha at almost every turn.

My flower offerings to Ganesha remind me of the beautiful, open-hearted people I met in India, especially the people at Parmarth Niketan Ashram. I often think of them as I adorn Ganesha's image with flowers. I *love* India.

Shiva is worshipped in Hindu traditions as the destroyer and restorer of worlds. Most images show him dancing. As a dancer, I relate to this image as the embodiment of eternity. I think of us all dancing through life in our own ways. The flowers I offer Shiva remind me that my journey with the flowers is my most sacred dance.

BOUQUETS TO ART

I consider my art to be a spiritual practice. It is a place where I connect deeply with the Creator. Museums, to me, are public altars of art. Many fine arts museums host yearly or biannual events spotlighting flowers. I have spoken and given demonstrations at such events in both Richmond, Virginia, and Boston.

I have also created floral offerings for the opening gala event for Bouquets to Art in San Francisco. Floral artists are invited to these events and assigned an object of art, which is to be the inspiration for their floral creation. At Bouquets to Art in 2002, I was given the honor of creating an offering to frame Rodin's *The Three Shades*.

The pieces were 16 ft (4.8 m) tall and housed in three-hundred-year-old vessels from China that were once used for shipping. They were created with all-white flowers, including calla lilies, hydrangea, roses, and Casablanca lilies. If you live near a major city, I suggest that you see if one of these events takes place in your local fine arts museum. It can be such a blessing to the soul.

❧ 3 ❧

Planting Seeds

As a child, I connected with the wonders of nature in my own first garden. I remember being amazed: how could that little wooden-like object called a seed produce the magic of a flower? This question was born anew each time a stalk reached out through the fragrant soil and toward the sun. My most colorful imaginings could not unravel the mystery of this small creation unfolding its fragile strength. Thankfully, this childlike wonder is still alive and thriving today and finds its way into my daily work.

It was the act of planting seeds that firmly rooted me into observing what was to unfold. I consider relationships to be much like planting seeds. The people I connect with, the relationships I nurture, are like the seeds I plant in the earth. Just as the seed unfolds into the plant, bringing beauty and joy into our lives, so have those relationships unfolded into unending gifts of beauty, joy, the sharing of personal wisdom, and letting go.

MEDITATION:

Water Flower

WE CAN PLANT all the seeds in the world, but they will not grow without the life-giving power of water. This meditation has been designed to honor the deep connection between water and the plant life it sustains.

Choose a single-stem flower that floats well, such as sunflowers or spider mums. Cut the length of the stem off so that just the flower head remains. Place the flower delicately against your heart. Feel the beat of your heart connecting you to the ancient connection of humans and flowers. Simply breathe and deeply feel this connection. Consciously infuse that flower with your intention or prayer.

After ten mindful breaths, place the flower gently on the surface of the water. Let go . . . just release that flower into the water. I prefer doing this meditation at a stream or creek, but any body of water will do. It can even be a simple bowl full of water. It is the release of the intention into the world that is the key here. You are essentially "planting the seed" of your intention.

FLOWERS FOR HEALING

The flowers in this photo were placed as part of a deep meditation
I offered when I found out that my friend Michael was very ill and in
the hospital. This was the first time that I created an offering in this
way. Each flower was placed with intent and reverence, calling for
my full presence and awareness in each moment. The full meditation lasted for two hours. This offering was done at The Sanctuary
at Omega Institute in upstate New York.

Seeds of Intention

AFTER I HAD MOVED from Los Angeles to Santa Cruz, California, to start my own floral business, Passionflora, my work took a new direction in 1995 when I was asked to create an altar space for Ram Dass, author of *Be Here Now*. He was so very kind, and I remember him saying that he did not feel worthy of sitting on the rather palatial environment that was created for him. Just hearing the love and devotion with which he spoke was so influential in directing my own journey with flowers.

At his speaking engagement that night, I made an affirmation to myself that continues to direct my life to this day. It was that I would be wide open to being asked to co-create with those whom I see as raising the vibration of the planet, and to be given opportunities to bring more love into this world in big ways. Six months later, I was asked to create the first of what would eventually be many flower offerings for His Holiness the Dalai Lama, for an event called "Peacemaking: The Power of Nonviolence." It was at that event when I first connected with Alice Walker, who remains someone who continually enriches my life by her presence, at times and in ways that only she can.

NEW YORK CITY

Around that same time, I was asked to create for an event featuring Maya Angelou, who has been such a phenomenal figure in my life. In 1998, I moved to New York City. Upon my arrival, I called her. Her kindness was instrumental in getting me started in New York.

My first job in the city was for the wedding of a couple of well-known actors. By 1999, I was creating for many celebrity-filled functions. At Bette Midler's New York Restoration Project, I was so very impressed when Bette showed up at nine o'clock in the morning wearing overalls, no makeup, and asking me to put her to work. I had to shoo her away. What a lovely lady she is.

OMEGA INSTITUTE
In the spring of 1999, I created for another event where Maya Angelou was the keynote speaker. At that event, I was invited to spend some time at the Omega Institute in upstate New York. Omega Institute is the world's leading holistic learning center and hosts about 23,000 people per season.

I arrived there in the fall of 1999 with an open mind and heart, ready to get out of the city. While there, I volunteered in the garden. I told the gardener I would help with the flower arrangements if needed. In 2000, I was asked to spend the full season at Omega, from March to October, creating flower offerings for all the workshops that were held there. I created about twenty pieces a week and also many floral sculptures in all sorts of spaces around the grounds.

I did this every year at Omega until 2012, and occasionally still offer my Being with Flowers workshops there. It was at Omega where I had the privilege of meeting so many wonderful people, people whose work helps raise the vibration of this planet.

"I perhaps owe having become a painter to flowers."
—CLAUDE MONET

DANCING WITH THE FLOWERS

One evening at Omega, I was having tea with a (then) member of Omega's board of directors, Linda Goldstein. She asked me what else I had done in my life besides work with flowers. I told her I had studied dance and was approaching the professional level when the flowers took over my life. She then told me she was singer Bobby McFerrin's manager. She said he was doing a show they called "What's Next," where he wouldn't know who was coming up onstage next to create with him.

We decided my offering would be the encore. It was the first time that I combined dance with floral arrangement onstage. Musician Michael Franti was a good friend of mine by that time, and he was in the audience that night at my invitation. He came up to me after the show and told me that he had been in tears the whole time I was onstage with Bobby, and would love it if I would do the same thing with his band, Spearhead.

Performing with Michael became a regular part of my work. After one of the first performances, the astounding drummer from the livetronica band Sound Tribe Sector 9, Zach Velmer, invited me to perform with his band as well. That, too, became a regular thing. At an after-party for a Sound Tribe Sector 9 show, I met the visionary electronic music producer Tipper and started working with him that night. I created for his full set, and his manager, Dave Veler, loved it so much that he asked me to create with Tipper at several more shows that year. This has led to further work with many musical acts across various genres.

That one moment with Linda Goldstein planted the seed for what would become a large part of the work I do today. I continue to co-create live floral arrangements at events and music festivals worldwide.

My work allows me to connect with people through the beauty of flowers. Often that connection is made by giving flowers to them, or by placing flowers in the spaces from which they will share their wisdom or their music. The deep blessing of sharing in this way happened routinely during my tenure at Omega. It was where I first connected with Eckhart Tolle, visionary artists Alex and Allyson Grey, Iyanla Vanzant, Deepak Chopra, Pema Chödrön, and many other notable figures.

"Deep in their roots, all flowers keep the light."

—THEODORE ROETHKE

Floral Wisdom

BEING FLOWERS

My dear sister-friend, the environmental activist Julia Butterfly Hill, shared with me a wonderful story about how flowers in her local landscape taught her a valuable lesson. She said, "I was marching back and forth, waiting for the train to come, and in my mind it was just all these negative thoughts, about what wasn't working, what was going wrong. Why, in this event that I was going to go do, why did they mess up all these logistics? I was just negative in my brain, and just so frustrated.

"Then, as I'm walking back and forth on the platform, all of a sudden, something catches my attention. And there are these little, tiny little spots of color, in between the gray concrete and the strip of metal that the train pulls up next to. And all of a sudden, it was the most important teacher of my day. And I literally knelt down and I started crying and I said, 'Thank you, flowers, thank you for teaching me.'

"And what they did in that moment was they made me realize how small my thoughts were making my world. That all I was caught up in were all the things that weren't working. And then here are all these little tiny flowers, growing up in a crack, in a crevice, where concrete meets metal. Where people stomp all over them all day, not even realizing that they're there, how much beauty they're bringing. And they're not sitting there moaning and complaining about the fact that they're stuck in a public transportation system instead of being out in a beautiful field with all the other flowers. They're just there, being flowers."

LIFE IS BEAUTIFUL

Hudson Soules showed up one day to help me create at a Spearhead concert. He was also an assistant to me at the Omega Institute in 2006. It has been my honor to watch him blossom and see the work that he is doing in the world. He has taken what I have shared with him and built on it, to make a living in landscaping and gardening.

He is also a DJ and, most of all, a fine human being with a kind heart and such a thoughtful way of communicating. We share much laughter. I am proud to call him my student and friend. My students are often my deepest teachers.

Hudson said, "Flowers remind me to be gentle and giving, as well as bold and subtle. As a professional gardener and landscaper, I have been privileged over the past eight years to be in the presence of many flowers, and have helped many grow. I recognize flowers as a terrestrial and cosmic sign that communicates beyond languages: *life is beautiful!*

"My friend Anthony shared with me, through example, how inspiring and healing being with flowers can be—working with and learning from them, rather than using them. The flowers themselves teach me about beauty, acceptance, giving, reciprocity, and healing.

"Beyond stopping to smell the flowers, Anthony taught me to listen to them and to be present with them. This awareness and respect for flowers is something I will always be grateful for and is a gift that is available to everyone."

THE SACRED GEOMETRIES OF FLOWERS

Visionary artists Alex Grey and his wife, Allyson, provide a clear and potent example for me and many others of what a truly evolved partnership looks and feels like. It is authentic.

Together, they are spearheading the building of Entheon, a structure that will house a work of his, titled *The Sacred Mirrors*, along with other works of deep meaning to the Love Tribe community. Please see www.cosm.org for more information.

Alex Grey, pictured below at left, has a wonderful way with words, and his deep, artistic views provide such a visionary way of seeing and relating our human connection with flowers: "And so the flower becomes like the momentary face of God that blasts us with its beauty. They're like raw beauty, you know? Why this beautiful? This strange? This bizarre? You know, some flowers are just bizarre. Some of them, orchids that look like Pekingese dogs—they're just weird.

"And then there are the sacred geometries of flowers. There are so many that are five-petaled, then the six-petaled, and so many that are all these innumerable petals. The Fibonacci spirals on the sunflowers and things. The spiral phyllotaxis of the growth of the leaves that are about to bud and fruit a flower.

"And then, with this offering to the world, this gift to the Sun, in a way, then all of the creatures come and enjoy it. The bees and the hummingbirds and the butterflies, all kinds of creatures, come and feed on the glory. The glorious beauty that is offered."

"They're the most natural epiphanies of the sacred that we have. I mean, here you are, you may be going along, in a depressed mood or whatever, and then BAM. And you always feel blessed by this. You always think, 'How did this beautiful, colorful thing come into my life?'"

—SAM KEEN

FLOWERS: THE CONSISTENT PRESENCE OF GOD'S LOVE

I have had the joy of seeing Iyanla Vanzant share her passion for helping people do better, feel better, and live better. She comes from that place of "I did it, and so can you." She helps us peel off our layers of self-doubt and apprehension. Iyanla says, "What I think that is transcendent about flowers, is that flowers represent the Creator's love for us. That no matter what season, no matter what location, no matter where you are, you can always find a flower of some kind. Some flower that's going to be blooming and growing, that you can take and use to remind yourself that the presence of love, the presence of the Creator, is always around us.

"The same rose that makes a bleeding heart at a funeral is the same rose that makes a bridal bouquet, or the same rose that brings sweethearts together, or the same rose that makes a dinner table look nice. Because love is consistent. And flowers, for me, are just the consistent presence of God's love.

"The most powerful messages that a flower can give us come from those little blooms, or clovers, or leaves, sometimes even blades of grass, that grow up between the concrete. We think that the concrete is so hard, and so heavy, and holds a place. But still, if you look in certain places, little flowers will just poke their tiny heads up."

Bulb Magic

WHEN THE EARTH is too solid and compacted from the cold weather, this next exercise will give you a magical preview of the beautiful spring that is to come. It is an especially wonderful gift to share with friends, particularly in locations where gardening in the soil outside is a very short-lived possibility.

Place rocks or marbles inside the various glass vessels, three-quarters of the way to the top. Fill the vessels with water until it reaches the top of the rocks or marbles.

Insert the bulbs snugly into the rocks or marbles, just below the surface. Be sure the tips of the bulbs rise out of both the rocks and water. Place in a closet or other dark, warm space.

MATERIALS

Decorative rocks
or marbles

Clear glass vessels,
varying sizes

Narcissus bulbs

Within weeks, there should be about 6"
(15 cm) of greenery. Remove the vessel
from the closet and place it in a lit area.
Keep water at the highest level possible,
just below the surface of the rocks.

Enjoy the fragrance of the flowers that will
bloom before your eyes.

❧ 4 ❦

Conscious Gathering

Every time I step outside and look up at the trees, it helps me tune in to a sense of childlike wonder. A flaming red leaf reaches out to brush my shoulder, and I smile because nature speaks so clearly. This is another type of voice, another kind of song. This is a dance I could dance forever and a song that will never be fully sung. For in this communion we are in the womb of life itself, and all else can melt away. Bringing this awareness into your own life is a powerful way to assist in lifting the vibration of our beautiful blue planet.

As Eckhart Tolle wrote in *A New Earth*, "Seeing beauty in a flower could awaken humans, however briefly, to the beauty that is an essential part of their own innermost being; their true nature. The first recognition of beauty was one of the most significant events in the evolution of human consciousness. The feelings of joy and love are intrinsically connected to that recognition."

MEDITATION:

Mindful Gathering

THE POWER OF nature is a guiding force for us all, whether we are aware of it or not. Of all my teachers, nature is my strongest. Take the time now to reflect on how nature has guided and influenced your life. What is your clearest and most powerful experience where nature was the teacher? I suggest you spend some of your sacred resource called time, and spend it alone—really alone, with no distraction, no other company—in nature. Give yourself this gift at least once a week.

This walking meditation has stops every fifteen to twenty steps, for about a minute. The goal is to stop and take in the sights, sounds, and smells right where you are, and then continue at a mindful pace. Please do not do this meditation in traffic! Being mindful means bringing a deep awareness to exactly where you are in any given moment.

For this meditation, you will need one 5 gal (19 L) bucket filled about 5 in (13 cm) deep with the freshest water possible and a pair of sharp clippers or pruners. Start outside in a place where you can walk safely. Take ten mindful breaths to fully arrive at a place of presence before you take the first step.

You should walk in a very slow and purposeful manner. After about twenty

tip

A fun way to complete this meditation is with at least one flower friend, and in silence. One person will carry the bell of mindfulness (any small bell with a pleasant sound will do) and will ring it to stop, and then ring it again when it is time to continue. This is especially nice to do with a group of flower friends, but all must remain silent the whole time.

"Earth laughs in flowers."

—RALPH WALDO EMERSON

steps, stop and take in the view. Check in with your senses. Breathe. You are alive! Look around. Is there anything there that you may not have ever noticed before? Something that could be worked into your creation?

Begin slowly walking again, stopping about every twenty steps for a short check-in and reassessment of your surroundings. Gather slowly. Each time you cut a flower, say, "Thank you, Earth."

You may want to walk for a full minute, but take time to periodically check in. If you feel your mind wandering away from the task at hand, breathe deeply ten more times and reset. When you feel as though you are really present, you may stretch out the frequency of your resting stops.

Always ask permission when you wish to create with flowers growing in someone's yard. This is a great way to meet your neighbors. It is also nice to gift them with a creation including some of their flowers.

tip

It is important to remain silent during this meditation. You may want to wear a badge that says "in silence." This will help others understand your silence.

Preparing to Create

BEFORE I BEGIN any piece, I start by acknowledging my senses. What do I smell? What can I taste? What sounds fill the air around me? How do the flowers feel to the skin on my hands? This recognition of the senses is a great way to ground you in the present moment.

The next step is to answer a few simple questions. What am I gathering for? Who will be viewing this? Where will the pieces live once they have been created? In answering these questions beforehand, I am equipped to gather only what I need. Part of being mindful is gathering only what you plan to work with and then working only with what you take.

Most important, gather from a place of gratitude and a willingness to be open to the sacred act of creation. At the end of gathering, say aloud or to yourself, "Thank you, Mother Earth." This deep "thank you" can also be an ongoing mantra.

For me, creation is often about surrender. It is the intuition of the grandmothers. It is the power of the present moment. Before you begin any creation, place your left hand on your heart, your right hand on top of your left. Lean your head back as far back as you can and look up toward the sky or ceiling. Contemplate the vastness of what is above you. Then slowly, mindfully, lower your head and gaze until you focus on the earth or floor below you. Breathe deeply ten times, as you gratefully and deeply feel that you are being held by Mother Earth. By doing this short meditation, you are now more prepared to create.

What is your creative process? Do you have one? If you don't, try the meditation I mention above. It could help you become radically *present*.

THIS MOMENT

This moment—this one and singular moment—is all we have. Flowers can bring us right into the moment in a most sweet and fragrant manner.

Gathering Materials

WHEN I CREATE, I never work with standard green floral foam. Never. Not only is it nonbiodegradable, but it is also made primarily of the carcinogenic ingredients formaldehyde and carbon black, along with other nasty things such as barium sulfate. Instead, I like to work with small, pliable branches or vines found close to where I live. When placed inside the vessel, the branches create the tension necessary to keep blooms and greenery in place.

Curly willow can be purchased or ordered from most places that sell flowers. If you do cut a branch from a tree or a flower from its home plant, always work in gratefulness. Be aware of what you are doing, and offer a prayer of gratitude to the plant that is offering so much to you. This simple practice can help deepen your connection with the garden we call Earth.

In addition to branches and vines, these are some of the other materials I often use:

- Glass vessels, various sizes
- Raffia or twine
- Stem tape
- An open mind and heart

A good paring knife or sharp pair of pruning clippers helps when it comes to making clean cuts into the stems or branches you work with. I like to work with a sharp pair of branch pruners for most of my offerings. For more delicate stems, I prefer a good pair of Japanese bonsai shears, although a sharp paring knife does the trick. I also recommend buying a pair of metal thorn strippers—they are invaluable.

I love to work with any vessel available, but I prefer glass vessels. I love to see the beauty within, created by the stems and branches—the roots of life. Any glass vessels in simple shapes will do. I like to employ bubble bowls of varying sizes, cylindrical and rectangular vases, and squat squares. A Mason jar also works in a pinch.

tip

Placing your vessel in the middle of a lazy Susan is a great way to ensure that your arrangement is consistent from all angles during creation.

I feel the most alluring flower arrangements are ones that appear to have been dug up in the wild and placed in a vessel. Sometimes to achieve this look, mechanics are required. When tying up stems or vines, you will need some type of twine. I like working with raffia as a tie instead of wire. It provides a more natural connection to one's work.

The most cherished way that I have gathered flowers is from gardens where I have planted them from seed. Having the time to plant and nurture the flowers for your creations is ideal. I hope you have the blessing of creating in this way at some point during your personal journey with the flowers.

I realize, however, that many people do not have the luxury of growing their own flowers. In this case, it is equally as important to be mindful of how you collect or purchase the flowers you create

with. In most cities' farmer's markets, there will often be at least one farmer selling flowers. This is a wonderful way to support local farmers and nurture a closer connection with the flowers you create with.

Get to know a local florist whose work speaks to you. Ask them where their flowers come from. Perhaps they can order some just for you. The Internet is also full of websites where you can find growers of organic flowers. Organic flowers clipped one day can be shipped to your home or office the next day. Get creative with your sources, but always be mindful of theirs.

tip

Choosing the correct vessel is like
choosing the correct outfit. One would
not wear jeans to a black-tie event.

5

The Art of Conscious Floral Arranging

My work is greatly influenced by the reverence I have for ikebana, the Japanese art of flower arranging. This deep and ancient practice is said to have originated in the Buddhist ritual of offering flowers to the dead. In the sixth century, Buddhism was introduced to the Japanese, and by the tenth century, the Japanese had elevated the offering from a few petals strewn around the altar to the use of containers for this work. Ikebana developed out of this practice, and although it was originally reserved for royalty and nobility, its presence during traditional festivals and exhibitions has ensured that ikebana is now widely appreciated by the general public.

MEDITATION:

Flower Dance

THE FLOWER DANCE MEDITATION is one way in which I believe it is possible to create real and sustained growth. It is a meditation during which some people will become uncomfortable. Breathing through your discomfort may help you expand your life experience. I realize there are those who do not understand *why* I dance with flowers. My response is, "If you are sitting there trying to figure out what I am doing, you may be missing the point." Allow yourself to approach this meditation from your heart and not your head.

There are the flowers, moving, spinning—it is creation in action. The merging of the fine arts of dance and floral arranging is something most people have never heard of. The only other person I have heard of creating in this art form was a man in fifth-century Japan. Someone brought his existence to my attention a full four years after I had been performing what I call Live Visionary Floral Sculpture.

To approach this meditation, one must have an open heart and mind. Let the flowers and other flora move through you and into the vessel. Be a channel of creation. Offer this, like all your work, as a selfless gift to the world.

Begin by setting the space with music that moves you. I think it is helpful when the music is without words—meaning instrumental music or even chanting, which is often words repeated in foreign languages. Please stand if you are able, although it is not necessary. Take a flower into your hand and simply let the music move your body.

Most music is devised with the rhythm of the heart in mind. If you feel self-conscious, it may be that you are thinking too much. Your movement will come from your instinct, if you will allow it. Just have fun and find your way to the vase when it feels right.

You can create a full arrangement with the same techniques I share with you here. Let the flowers guide your movements, be aware of spacing, and most importantly, have fun! The arrangement will come to life before your eyes. Your deeply present attention and sense of joy as you move and create will be evident in the final product.

note

Many of my live offerings can be watched on YouTube. Do a search for "BeingwithFlowers Anthony Ward."

Floreography

THE WORD *floreography* came to me through a wordsmith that I know. It was his way of describing certain moves that I make when I am dancing with the flowers. I believe it is more than just a word, however. It is something that each of us can evolve into as we continue our own dance.

I often share my work with the flowers live on stage, creating floral sculptures with either live musicians or, as in the case of most of the music festivals at which I perform, with musicians who specialize in what I like to call Visionary Electronic Music, or VEM. This music is more commonly referred to as Electronic Dance Music, or EDM, but I feel that it is much more than just dance music. Most of it is created with an intentionally higher vibration, and the music is designed to help listeners go deep within their own spiritual selves. Some of my main collaborators in this genre of music are Tipper, Desert Dwellers, Bluetech, Random Rab, Love and Light, Emancipator, and OTT.

I have also created many times with Michael Franti and Spearhead. The music of any genre that moves me becomes an open invitation for co-creation to occur. The flowers and I have created on stage with Indian devotional chant masters Deva Premal & Miten and Snatam Kaur, Native American flautist R. Carlos Nakai, Tibetan flute player and composer Nawang Khechog, and world-renowned classical pianist Katya Grineva.

On many inspiring occasions, I have also performed in the company of my friends, visionary artists Alex and Allyson Grey. On some of these occasions, we have been bathed in the glory of the light, color, and sacred geometry of visionary digital artists Andrew "Android" Jones and Jonathan Singer. These performances are such an important part of my journey with the flowers. They have infused my work with new and vital energy.

In your own work with the flowers, it is incumbent upon you to bring your full life experience to the arranging table. What are other ways in which you are a creative force in this world? Only you can really answer this. Bring this passion, along with all your heart and soul, to every precious experience you have with the flowers.

My very first creative expression involved the movement of my body. Being in a family with eight kids, my way of gaining positive attention was to dance. Whenever we had company, my dad would have me "put on a floor show." There was a time in my life that I lived for Saturday mornings, when the show *Soul Train* was my heaven on earth. All these stylish black kids on TV, dancing with so much grace, joy, and ancient soul-stirring rhythm, was a blessed occurrence in my life. This was "dance church," if you will.

This passion led to my study of ballet and modern dance at the Lompoc School of Dance in California, where my dance teacher, Denise Donlon, was a gifted student of teachers who had studied with the New York City Ballet. I easily equate ballet with ikebana. I consider ikebana to be the ballet of floral arrangement. Ballet legend Mikhail Baryshnikov was known to go to the barre every day and practice the basics of ballet, even at the height of

his career. Like practicing at the barre in ballet, ikebana is a practice, and there is structure in the practice.

I keep a few books on ikebana that are from Japan as my holy books. I do not speak or read Japanese, but these books are done in such a manner that I am able to understand and embody this practice. I have no formal training in ikebana, but at a very key time in my journey with the flowers I spent an hour in silence every morning for a year, creating a small piece working with this mindful technique. I have been told many times by Japanese people that my work is "Japanese style." I take this as a huge compliment.

If you wish to approach your work with the flowers in a conscious manner, find books on the philosophy and practice of ikebana. Your local library will be helpful in this. Ikebana is a disciplined art form, where the arrangement itself is a living thing. Spend some time developing an understanding of this tradition, for it is a spiritual practice, and can help you take your journey with the flowers to a deeper place.

Basic Rules of Conscious Floral Arrangement

TO PRACTICE the art of conscious flower arranging, we must be present before we begin the act of creation. Awareness of our intention for the offering is most helpful. Staying open to the moment-by-moment process is most vital. Focus. As little distraction as possible will guide your movement. Silence, when possible, is golden!

Working with the natural items available in your area can be a guidepost to the work you create in a conscious manner. I live in an area lush with moss, ivy, ferns, both evergreen and deciduous trees, and a host of native grasses. Pairing the natural flora of your area with cut organic flowers is one way to arrange in a conscious manner. This may not seem possible to some, but as you start to observe the world around you in the present moment, you may find more to work with than you expected.

Before there is a floral arrangement of any kind, there is water. Take a moment to acknowledge the water. It is perhaps the most precious of the

"Within the empty vessel exists the universe of possibilities."

—ANTHONY WARD

resources on our planet. Having fresh unfettered water to create with is nothing short of a luxury. Be aware of this blessing.

Whatever the vessel you work with, fill it with water to about ½ in (1 cm) from the top. Acknowledge this water blessing by placing your hands on the vessel and infusing it with your grateful awareness. Please take some time before you begin to simply breathe in the possibilities.

In the interior of the vessel we will build the skeleton, to create a welcoming environment for the flowers you will arrange. Choose pliable branches— curly willow is my favorite for this purpose. It has clean, smooth skin, and sometimes the stems can be replanted after the arrangement is transitioned. Grape vine, when stripped of loose skin, also makes an excellent interior. Birch

branches are striking and effective for this key step as well.

As I said before, I do not work with floral foam. When I first began my professional career, I worked at an upscale floral shop in a trendy part of Los Angeles. The owner did a large volume of work and regularly had people working with floral foam. I read on the box that it is carcinogenic and harmful to pregnant women, and I vowed at that moment to never work with it. I wanted to find ways to work with organic materials instead. I cringe when I see floral designers demonstrating how to work with floral foam, and I challenge the makers of these products to come up with something else that is both earth- and people-friendly. It is time to clean up this aspect of the industry!

Preparing the flowers you will create with is a key step in conscious arranging. Each flower should have its stem sliced about ¼ in (6.4 mm) at the bottom, right up the middle, to ensure the flower drinks. Flowers must drink to stay more viable in the water, which is another reason to avoid floral foam. The size and shape of the vessel will determine the final stem length of the offering you create. I like to separate the collected greenery and flowers and place them in water to keep them fresh as we work together.

I find it most desirable to work with odd numbers when creating any arrangement. Think of the vessel separated in that way as well. When creating an arrangement that is designed to live against a wall, keep in mind the three-quarters of the vessel that will be viewed, but remember that there should be movement in the back of the vessel as well, just enough so that the back of the arrangement does not appear flat. I like to work on a lazy Susan to ensure the work is balanced in all directions.

Observe, both in the garden and in nature, how the foliage, vines, grasses, and flowers grow in their natural setting. In your offerings, work with them in this natural manner, as a way to honor these glorious gifts we are given.

I do not profess that this way of creating is the only way for you to deepen your own relationship with flowers. In my life, it is during the act of creating where I have found the most personal growth. I have rooted my awareness in both observation and silence. For me, this calling is my daily spiritual practice.

note

Hollow stems, such as those of delphiniums, will not need to be split up the center because they drink their water through the hollow opening.

Classical Arrangement

CLASSICAL ARRANGEMENTS often bring to mind the lushness of English country gardens and the still-life paintings of the Dutch Masters. Some of my favorites are Vermeer, Paulus Theodorus van Brussel, Abraham Mignon, and Rachel Ruysch.

Place the trumpet vase in the large fruit bowl so that it is centered and stable. Secure the curly willow inside the vase.

Add the grapes by securing them with raffia and then add the eucalyptus and other greens. Work with them as they grow in nature. Follow the arches and contours of each stem.

MATERIALS

10" (25.5 cm) trumpet vase

Large fruit bowl with flat bottom to hold vase

Curly willow

Four plump clusters of green grapes (organic when possible)

Raffia

Five arching branches of seeded eucalyptus

Variegated ivy

One ten-stem bunch of leucadendron

Nine hot pink roses

Autumnal nandina leaves

One ripe vine of three tomatoes, on the stem (organic when possible)

One bunch of alstroemeria

One bunch of pink waxflower

Irish broom

Three branches of privet berries

Three nandina berry clusters

One five-stem bunch of hot pink gerbera daisies

Five water tubes

Incorporate leucadendron into the center and evenly around the mouth, following its natural growth pattern.

Place the roses front and center in a cluster. Add autumnal nandina leaves around the center of the vessel. Add the branch of tomatoes to the front left.

The alstroemeria should be just above the roses but also interacting with them.

Place the waxflowers between the roses and alstroemeria. This arrangement can serve as a complete classical piece.

The incorporation of Irish broom adds a modern edge to this classical piece.

"Flowers are the manifestation of love itself."

—ANTHONY WARD

For a still-life painting effect, complete the offering with the berries. Secure the gerbera daisies in the water tubes and rest them on the berries.

Modern Arrangement

MODERN ARRANGEMENTS speak to me of dramatic focused movement, clean lines, and spare elements. One element that I find crucial in these pieces is bear grass, also sometimes called Indian basket grass. It is extremely pliable and will last much longer than most flowers. You can give it a fresh cut and work with it again. Clear glass vessels in simple shapes—square, spherical, or cylindrical—lend themselves well to these edgy creations.

Place one vessel in each quadrant of the table upon which you are creating your offering.

Loop the bear grass inside the glass vessels to create a base for the flowers and a circular movement in these minimalist offerings.

Add wheatgrass to the smallest vessel and horsetail to the largest. Plase the daisies into the bear grasses of the smaller vessels.

MATERIALS

Three square glass vessels in
varying heights

One 18" (45.5 cm) cone-
shaped vessel

Bear grass

Wheatgrass

Horsetail

White gerbera daisies with black
centers

Variegated aspidistra leaves

Blue thistle

Bells of Ireland

Birds of paradise

Arrange the aspidistra, at a
slightly upward angle, around the
mouth of the vessel. Blue thistle
and bells of Ireland are arranged
at the top of the offering.

Add one bird of paradise, to
conjure the image of a bird.

In the rectangular vessel
below, add three more birds
of paradise.

The Super Natural

THE PAIRING OF large gems, geodes, and other brilliant stones with flowers and feathers offers us the awareness of the deep testament of beauty our planet gifts to us. I call these more unusual arrangements "Super Natural."

Various-sized orchids help strike an organic balance. Two orchids were footed by low arrangements of blue thistle and tea leaves. The center orchid was submerged in a wooden treasure box.

These amethyst geodes weigh about 200 lb (91 kg) each. I placed orchid heads where they rested comfortably with no mechanics. Bells of Ireland in water tubes were added to the middle.

I first created in this way when I was asked to create floral pieces to frame the stage of my favorite livetronica band Sound Tribe Sector 9. The band had a crew of people who had volunteered to bring in some gigantic crystals. It took three strong men to lift one onto the stage. I would incorporate my work with the flowers into these giant crystals as my offering. The result seemed to enliven the audience in an almost super-natural way, even before the amazing music started.

As Eckhart Tolle says in *A New Earth*, "Since time immemorial, flow-ers, crystals, precious stones, and birds have held special significance for the human spirit . . . Their special

A pared-down presentation of the same offering, showcasing the geodes.

The center quartz stone is 3½' (1 m) tall. The roughness of the smaller quartz on the sides offer a nice contrast to the center.

significance and the reason why humans feel such fascination for and affinity with them can be attributed to their ethereal quality."

The following is an example of an installation piece, reminiscent of what I create to adorn the stages of Sound Tribe Sector 9. I hope it will inspire you to bring the magic of gems into your life and pair them with flowers. The combination of these magical earth gifts is a particularly powerful inspiration in my life.

In keeping with the forest vibe of this offering, I added horsetail, ferns, and evergreen branches.

The foreground and vessels were populated with an abundance of oriental lilies in various states of opening.

The centerpiece also housed white stock, aspidistra, and privet berry.

I am told this clustered quartz geode takes five strong men to lift it. Nine white roses were placed in welcoming spots on the surface of the geode.

6

Celebrations of Life

Life is a precious gift, although it does not always feel like it. Sometimes we are pulled into dramas that make life seem difficult to bear. At these times, I feel it is important to consider the alternative to life, which is death.

Whatever we are going through attaches us to life. This itself is cause for celebration. I am often asked to help people mark important life events by creating flower offerings to adorn these gatherings. I hold these experiences so very dear. It is such an honor to be asked to share my art at these important occasions.

Throughout history and around the world, flowers can be found at almost every human celebration of life's passages. They help bring beauty, awareness, color, and scent to our lives. They enrich our memories and enliven our spirits as we celebrate together with family and friends. Your work with the flowers can be a wonderful contribution to the celebrations in your life.

MEDITATION:
Ancestral Flower

WHEN I GOT MY first job as a teenager, I made it a ritual to buy my mother flowers every payday. She said how much she appreciated me giving her flowers while she was alive to enjoy them. Flowers certainly are for the living, but they can also be a deep way of remembering and connecting to the memories and energy of those who are dear to us who have departed. The Ancestral Flower meditation can be a very simple yet profound way for you to do this.

We typically think of an ancestor as one who is from the generation before our grandparents, but anyone who has come before us is also an ancestor. For this meditation, please pick someone special to you who has departed this world. Choose a single bloom, perhaps one your ancestor particularly enjoyed.

Now it is time to hold the flower gently, breathe easily, and recall a story, a feeling, or perhaps even a sound that helps bring the person into your heart and your vastly opened mind. Maybe you have a picture of this person, which would be helpful in bringing your full attention to the present. It is a time in honor and remembrance of this person who has come before you.

Do you remember their laughter? Is there a story you were told about them that connects you to them in a special way? Allow this meditation to bring you a sense of connection with your ancestor.

When Alice Walker was asked if she felt that she owed her fans another book like her best-selling, Pulitzer Prize–winning novel *The Color Purple*, she is known to have said, "No, I don't think I owe them anything. I owe my ancestors everything, though."

Flowers can be a deep way of remembering and connecting to the memories and energy of those who are dear to us who have departed.

—ANTHONY WARD

While still gently holding the flower and enjoying all it is offering you, please close your eyes and be open to what comes up for you. This meditation can also be a time to release any internally held resentment or unfinished business. For twenty mindful breaths, allow yourself to connect with what this person brought to your life.

Many of our ancestors suffered great hardship and challenge. It is both because of the pain they endured and also the hope they held for future generations that we are here and able to enjoy the Earth's abundant gift of flowers. When you are finished with this meditation, please place this flower on your personal altar.

Creating for Holidays: The Four Seasons

THE PASSAGE OF TIME in our lives is dotted with special events that are both traditional and cyclical, marked by the changing of weather and the length of daylight. Many people celebrate these changing seasons by adorning their homes and lives with nature and representative ornamentation.

Fill the vessel with water, place in a retaining vessel, and camouflage with moss. Begin to incorporate the daffodils.

Prune any dead leaves, but leave some of the foliage to create a natural look. Place them in a casual manner into the vessel.

Place blue thistle at varying levels inside the daffodil arrangement.

SPRING

ARRANGEMENT:
SPRING AWAKENING

As Earth renews and reawakens, we witness delicate, often fragrant flowers blossom on naked fruit tree branches while dormant bulbs break through moist soil. All at once, we are aware that Spring is here.

Before beginning this arrangement, remove the binding or rubber band from the daffodils. Give them a fresh cut at the base and then split the stem from the bottom up, about ¼ in (6 mm).

MATERIALS

Vessel large enough to hold the daffodils in a tight but manageable structure

Retaining vessel large enough to hold glass vessel

Mood moss

Three five-stem bunches of daffodils

One bunch (ten stems) blue thistle

Bush ivy with berries

Native grasses

Eighteen eggs

Insert bush ivy around the mouth of the vessel. Add grasses to give the feeling of a meadow setting.

To complete the offering, place eggs on moss around the base as a reminder of the potent rebirth aspect of spring.

SUMMER

ARRANGEMENT:
FLOWERS FOR MOM

Every living being has a mother, and flowers are a wonderful way to celebrate this special person in your life. The role of mother is not always a biological one—I have been called a "spiritual mother" by some very special people in my life. We all possess a nurturing spirit within us that can be cultivated and shared with others.

Before starting this offering, focus your awareness on the person for whom you are creating. Take a moment to reflect on how this person mothers you and how this affects your life.

Place tulips, curly willow, and privet berries into the water-filled vessel, according to the way their stems arch. Vertical stems work best in the center of the arrangement.

Add ivy leaves around the mouth of the vessel, and place sugar maple leaves so that they appear as if they are interacting with the tulips.

MATERIALS

Vessel

One bunch of white tulips

Curly willow, grape vine,
or pliable branches

Three clusters of privet berry

Variegated ivy

Sugar maple leaves

Variegated aspidistra

Seeded eucalyptus

One bunch of blush pink mini calla
lilies

Three stems of oriental lilies

One bunch of blue thistle

One bunch of pink alstroemeria

Native grasses

Add aspidistra and eucalyptus to the mouth of the vessel. Allow the eucalyptus to hang. Wind ivy up the curly willow branches. Add calla lilies in foreground; incorporate oriental lilies into the upper section.

For contrast, add blue thistle and pink alstroemeria. Adorn with native grasses as a finishing touch.

FALL

ARRANGEMENT:
HARVEST ABUNDANCE

The time of harvest is often equated with abundance and the gathering to offer thanks not only for the abundance but also for life itself. One such harvest celebration in America is Thanksgiving. It is my favorite American holiday. Creating centerpieces for Thanksgiving dinner at the home of my sister, Denise, her husband, Bob, and my nephew, A.J., has become a yearly tradition.

Working with a gourd or pumpkin as the vessel for your harvest centerpiece is such a fun way to celebrate this time of year. I hope you will experiment and make your own. You don't have to wait, because every meal can be an opportunity to give thanks.

"Autumn is the second spring when every leaf is a flower."
—ALBERT CAMUS

Hollow out the pumpkin and secure the vessel inside. Make the opening just large enough so that the vessel fits snugly.

Add rosehips to set up the mid-structure of the piece.

Add ivy, grapes, and sugar maple leaves to create a frame for the placement of the flowers.

MATERIALS

One 8" x 10" (20.5 x 25.5 cm)
round pumpkin (This can also be done
with melons.)

One watertight vessel to insert
into the pumpkin

One ten-stem bunch of rosehips

Ivy

Grape clusters (organic when possible)

Sugar maple leaves in
autumnal states of coloration

One dozen yellow roses

One ten-stem bunch yellow
alstroemeria

Native grasses

Odontoglossum orchid

Candles

Mixture of ornamental and
edible squashes

Incorporate yellow roses, alstroemeria,
and native grasses.

Add the odontoglossum orchid, candles, and
ornamental squash to create an abundant
offering. Fill the vessel with water.

WINTER

ARRANGEMENT:
WINTER FOREST

The view from my window is a sea of towering evergreen trees. Many of those trees are commonly associated with the winter holiday season. Their sweet, heady smell invites us to realize that it's that time of year when winter gatherings and holiday traditions are upon us. Creating an offering with evergreen branches will bring that fragrance into your living space. This offering can serve as a reminder that this sometimes solemn and less sunlit time of year is still a true beauty to behold.

Fill the vessel with a curly willow interior and garland it with green ivy. Place it on a bed of moss.

Add variegated ivy to the arrangement for a striking contrast.

MATERIALS

8" (20.5 cm) bubble
bowl vessel

Curly willow

Moss

Ivy, both green and variegated

Large crystal or stone

Evergreen branches

White poinsettia
as a cut flower

Cotoneaster bush
with red berries

Red roses

Votive candle in a
frosted vessel

Candle goblet of mosaic
cut glass

Place a large crystal so that it appears
as though the offering is growing from
its center.

Add evergreen branches and white
cut poinsettia for fragrance and to
establish height.

Cotoneaster with red berries can be arranged to create more contrast. Its striking red berries add dimension.

Red roses become the focal point of this holiday offering.

"The temple bell stops, but I still hear the sound coming out of the flowers."

—BASHO

Candlelight, in a frosted vessel, adds context to the piece as a reminder of the weather and darkness outside. It is a reminder to keep the light burning within.

An additional candle goblet, in rich green mosaic cut glass, completes the offering.

ARRANGEMENT:
FOR ROMANCE

Nothing really says romance like honesty and thoughtfulness. Flowers can help bring this authentic expression to heart-centered and deep communication with your loved one. This romantic offering was completed with personal items that help bring the intimacy that fuels real romance.

Fill the vessel with water. Place the geodes on either side of it. Wind grape vines down into the interior of the vessel.

Place the grapes so that they cascade naturally around the mouth of the vessel. Attach them to the grape vine with raffia.

Place ivy around the outside of the vessel as it would grow in the wild. Follow the curves and arches to create a natural look.

MATERIALS

Vessel

Amethyst geodes to complement the size and shape of the vessel

Grape vine for vessel interior

Three robust bunches of organic grapes, if possible

Raffia

One bunch (about five medium-length strands) variegated ivy

Three hardy sugar maple branches (or substitute with whatever trees are local and abundant)

Eighteen-count bunch of American beauty roses or what is available or special to you

Nandina berries

Place the three sugar maple branches in a way that evokes the feel of a tree. When working with these elements, honor them by mirroring their growth in the natural world.

Add the roses, following the pattern you have created with the ivy and branches. Nandina berries are incorporated to further frame the flowers.

Creating for Weddings

THE FIRST TIME I was asked to create for a wedding, in 1994, I knew that it marked a momentous occasion along my journey with the flowers. I decided to partake in a ten-day fast to deepen both my preparation and my experience of the event. The couple was middle-aged and both had been married before, so they brought to the table experience and wisdom in what they hoped I would create for them. What I took away from that important event was to be as open and present during these creations as I strive always to be in life.

I create for the weddings of people from all walks of life—rich or poor, gay or straight. If there is a wedding theme, it is important to be clear on how literally the couple wants to stick to it. I like to find out what, if any, is a favorite flower or combination of flowers and make that the focal point.

I once created for a bride who wanted peonies and tuber roses, but had been advised by others that this combination was really not possible. My answer was, "This is your special day. You will have your request." It's always most important that the bride be happy with the results. This particular wedding was one of my first jobs in New York City, and the bride was overwhelmed with joy. The Associated Press reported that the reception looked like a scene out of the iconic film *Casablanca*.

"Love is the flower you've got to let grow."

—JOHN LENNON

TIPS FOR A SMOOTH WEDDING DAY

1. Always have extra flowers on hand for unexpected last-minute requests. You never know when you may need to create something for an unexpected family member.

2. Have at least three extra reception table arrangements prepared for unexpected arrivals. These can always be placed elsewhere if needed.

3. Give yourself more than enough time to arrive at the venue.

4. Enjoy the process, and aim to be a calming presence on the day of the event.

THE WEDDING OF MICHAEL FRANTI AND SARA AGAH

I first met singer-songwriter and social activist Michael Franti in Santa Cruz, California, while I was leaving flowers for him in his dressing room at a Spearhead concert in 1997. He was really touched and gave me a loving hug. I was so surprised when he came out onstage—he brought the flowers out and placed them on the keyboard. I must admit that although I was happy he wanted to share them, I spent much of the concert just hoping they would not fall over and get all the electrical things wet! Thankfully, they did not, despite all of the jumping around on stage.

When the show was over, Michael came out into the audience, as he always does when time permits. He grabbed my hand and said he wanted me to meet his manager. She asked if I would be into adorning the stage with flowers for the band the following week. Well, I was due to be in New York the next week and told her that I would not be able to because of that. She said they would be in New York that week as well, so how about then?

That night, a long and flower-filled connection with Michael began. Our timing would turn out to be very in sync, such as when we all happened to be in Paris at the same time in 2006.

Michael's band Spearhead was the second musical act that I ever created with live on stage. He also invited me to create with them at two of President Obama's Inaugural Balls, the Green Ball and the Peace Ball.

Creating with Michael and Spearhead has been an answered prayer, a prayer that is ongoing in my life. I ask that I be given the chance to co-create with those who are uplifting our planet and its people. I always tell people that, for me, Michael is a bright and clear example of a musician who is bravely and lovingly carrying the torch for musicians like John Lennon and Bob Marley. He brings so much joy to the world with his music and his kind heart.

When he told me he was going to be married and that it had always been his dream to have me create flower offerings for his wedding, I was only able to say that this was my dream as well. When I met his partner, Sara, I became even more excited and honored to be a part of their sacred ceremony. She is truly an amazing human being, and a wonderful match for Michael.

The two-day event took place in San Francisco, and I must say that in all my years of creating for weddings, this is the wedding I am so very happy to share with you in the pages of this book. It was, without a doubt, the most profound, sweet, heartfelt wedding I

"Every flower's got a right to be bloomin'."

—MICHAEL FRANTI

have been privileged to create for. At the cocktail party the night before the wedding ceremony, I offered a flower dance especially created for that night's gathering. It was a Bali-themed party, as Michael and Sara have a place in Bali where they love to spend time. We all wore white clothing, and I created with flowers in sunset tones.

With the graceful help of my dear friends and flower assistants Hudson and Sebastian, the wedding day was one of complete focus and joyful movement toward the six o'clock ceremony. I began that day at five in the morning. I love to rise early and spend

time enjoying the journey to those special moments.

When Michael told me that Sara loved her bouquet, I felt assured that all was better than well. The ceremony was simple and performed in the tradition of the Baha'i faith. The reception changeover went smoothly and so I became a guest at dinner, which is a rare thing. I love being the hired help and on very few occasions have I crossed the line of sitting down to dinner. This photographer, Jeff Marsh, consented to share one of the magical moments, which I am so very happy to present above.

THE BRIDAL BOUQUET

In my experience, the bridal bouquet is one of the most important aspects of a successful wedding. If the bride is happy with her bouquet, the chances for a successful event are much higher.

When making bouquets for the bridesmaids, create smaller versions of the bride's bouquet. Sometimes the bride may want to incorporate the colors of her bridesmaids' gowns or the theme of the wedding. The theme for this wedding was "Winter Forest."

When I create bridal bouquets, I usually do it all in my hands. For the purposes of this book, however, I have shown how the bouquet can be created within a vase and then removed for the final binding of the stems.

Loop aspidistra leaves through the evergreen branch and fasten them with stem tape.

Place the eucalyptus, oriental lilies, and mini callas inside the evergreen branch.

MATERIALS

Seven variegated aspidistra leaves

One cascading evergreen branch

Stem tape

Three seeded eucalyptus branches

Three white oriental lilies

Five blush pink mini calla lilies

Fifteen white roses

Three stems variegated ivy

Raffia

White satin ribbon

Cluster the roses to create lushness in the center of the bouquet. Place ivy in three spots around the roses to encircle the bouquet. Tie with raffia.

Bind the stems with satin ribbon to complement the bridal gown.

WEDDING MANDALA

The mandala is a spiritual and ritual symbol that represents the Universe in a metaphysical way. It is meant to convey a microcosm of the Universe. It is also an ephemeral way of connecting with eternity. Flowers lend themselves well to this simple yet lovely expression of the cyclical nature of our lives.

At a recent wedding for which I created flower offerings, the couple wanted a way that their guests could offer a prayer for their union in an inter-active manner. We came up with the idea of handing a flower to guests as they arrived, and asked them to place it on a specific spot in the design of a flower mandala, with good wishes for the couple's union.

You will need to find a spot where it can stay throughout the wedding, pref-erably where there is no chance of wind or other disturbances. At the comple-tion of the mandala, guests held hands around it and offered verbal wishes. The mandala presented here is an example of what was created that special day.

Create a 3' x 5' (0.9 x 1.5 m) bed of moss. Place a heart-shaped vessel filled with green pompom chrysanthemums in the center of the moss to anchor the creation.

MATERIALS

Mood moss

One open-faced heart-shaped vessel

One bunch green pompom
chrysanthemums

One bunch magenta pompom
chrysanthemums

One seven-stem bunch of sunflowers

Three aspidistra leaves

One bunch white pompom chrysanthemums

One bunch craspedia

Flattened glass marbles

One cymbidium orchid spray

Four stems of daffodils

Place three magenta chrysanthemums,
three sunflowers, and three aspidistra
leaves in a triangular pattern around the
heart-shaped vessel.

Arrange nine white chrysanthemums in line
with the sunflowers, following their triangular pattern. Place the sunflower heads at
the end of the chrysanthemums. Incorporate
white and magenta chrysanthemums into
the aspidistra leaves.

Evenly distribute the craspedia among the green mums. Incorporate magenta chrysanthemums around all sunflowers, in the center and outside edge. Alternate with white chrysanthemums. Place flattened marbles in the center of each sunflower.

Place cymbidium orchids in a triangular pattern, starting at the outermost edge of the mandala. Add daffodils in the lower quadrants around the vessel, next to the magenta chrysanthemums.

Finish placing cymbidium orchids in a triangular pattern around the outside of the flowers.

note

Cut the stems off the flowers all the way to the heads. Float the flower heads in water overnight to help them retain their freshness before placing them in the mandala. This is best done the night before the event.

Add a sunflower in the center of the heart-shaped vessel.
Place a flattened marble in the center of the sunflower.

Creating for Memorial Services

THE LIFE FORCE of all living beings will leave the bodies they inhabit and go into the mystery of death. For those of us fortunate enough to have family and community that will miss us when we die, some sort of gathering usually occurs. These gatherings are often called funerals, memorial services, or sometimes life celebrations. This transition will happen to you, me, and every person we know.

On many occasions, I have been asked to create flower offerings for these types of gatherings. I ask as much as I can about the deceased whenever possible. These celebrations are a visual and cathartic way of remembering the departed, so try to get as many details as possible about the individual and work in that spirit.

I recently read about a friend who had some houseguests. One of the guests was scheduled for a doctor's appointment the next day. After a nice meal, they all went to sleep. The appointment was set for 8 a.m. When they checked her room in the morning she was still asleep, so they just let her stay there. About an hour later, they checked again. This time they went in to find she was no longer among the living. This is perhaps the gentlest way to go—in one's sleep. But like being born, it is most often not our choice of how or when we depart. Do not take your life and the time you are given for granted. Celebrate it.

*Memorial celebrations are a
visual and cathartic way of
remembering the departed.*

The memorial flower offering on the following pages was created in remembrance of the esteemed visionary artist Robert Venosa. I had the joy of meeting him and his lovely wife Martina Hoffmann—also a renowned visionary artist—at the Omega Institute in upstate New York. They first came to Omega in 2006 to teach a workshop called "Painting the Fantastic," where they taught different techniques and deeper ways of being a more fully realized artist.

We made a yearly tradition of meeting at least one night during the week of their stay to share a bottle of red wine among the three of us. They would visit me in my rustic cabin, which I had nicknamed "The Studio." On one occasion, Robert noticed a gourd I had placed on the side table and asked me to bring it to their workshop space. He said he saw something there in the gourd. I brought it over the next day and he proceeded to paint a wizard's face in the mottled brown skin of the gourd. It appeared to have always been there. That piece will be on display at the Chapel of Sacred Mirrors Art Sanctuary of Alex and Allyson Grey. This memorial celebrates that part of Robert that lives and breathes, his beautiful wife Martina. She is symbolized by the orchid, which is the focal point of the offering.

MEMORIAL FLORAL SCULPTURE WITH ALTAR

The spiral vessel enclosure for the piece has an ethereal, light-filled quality, which is reminiscent of Robert's work. I realize that not everyone has a specialty item exactly like this. The idea here is to find something for the enclosure that will honor the essence of the person being memorialized.

MATERIALS

One ten-stem bunch of curly willow, each one 2' (61 cm) in length

One striking vessel enclosure

Bear grass

One large, fully flowered cymbidium orchid spray

Five stalks of horsetail

Five fern fronds

Three happy bamboo plants (shown with silver adornment in a 12" [30.5 cm] cylinder vessel)

Spiral fossil

Candle

Mosaic vessels

One white hydrangea

Fully opened "Bulb Magic" piece from chapter 3 (shown in the 6" [15 cm] bubble bowl)

One gourd

Any additional personal items that honor the departed

Wind the curly willow down into the empty vessel to create a structure for the flower placement.

Loop the bear grass around the outer vessel at varying levels to add volume and circular movement.

Position the cymbidium spray in the center of the vessel and secure.

Add horsetail and fern fronds to frame the orchid spray.

Place the happy bamboo display and spiral fossil to begin creating the full altar.

Place a candle in one mosaic vessel and the white hydrangea in the other. Add the mosaic vessels, "Bulb Magic" piece, and gourd.

Add any personal items that reflect the spirit of the person being memorialized. This altar includes a bookmark of Robert's painting *Buddhasphinx*, given to me by Robert before he passed.

7

Being with Flowers

In 2000, after a full season creating flower offerings for all of the workshops that took place at the Omega Institute, the world's leading holistic learning center located in upstate New York, I proposed teaching my own workshop there. To my great joy, the proposal was accepted. I spent a portion of every year for the next twelve years as an artist-in-residence at Omega. Each summer, I would teach my weekend-long workshop at least once.

In the following pages, I share with you some of this step-by-step workshop. I would certainly love to see each of you in person at one of the workshops I still hold. I would also love to hear about you, your friends, and your community creating and sharing your own Being with Flowers workshops. Like this book, my workshops are one of my gifts to the world. They will be here long after I am not.

MEDITATION:

Flower Insight

THE FLOWER INSIGHT MEDITATION is an expansion of the Single Flower meditation offered in chapter 1. In this situation, it is performed at the end of your day, as the last thing you do before you drift off to sleep. It is an opportunity to bring yourself to that very peaceful state that being with flowers offers us all.

Please choose a single bloom and place it in a bud vase. At a time when you can be alone just before you go to sleep, spend your last waking moments with that flower for ten minutes. This is a silent practice. Allow this flower to become your world. Simply breathe and be present.

Be open to this gift of silence and beauty. Let the flower help you see that taking in beauty is a healing way to relate to the world around you. Breathe in and out in a mindful manner while contemplating the flower for the last ten minutes before you turn off the lights. Place the bud vase near where you sleep. Let this calm beauty help you drift off into a deep and restful sleep.

The Workshop

A FEW DAYS BEFORE I taught my workshop for the first time, I began to feel a little stressed about really wanting to give the people who were arranging their lives, spending their money, and traveling from far and wide to attend my workshop something that could really lift them, something they could take home and have for the rest of their lives. I decided to take a silent walk alone on the beautiful trails that surround Omega, something I often did during my twelve-year tenure there. When I returned to my cabin, "The Studio," I sat down and wrote out, step by step, how I would arrange and teach the workshop.

I have also shared versions of it at Kripalu Yoga Center in Massachusetts, Mount Madonna Institute in California, the Museum of Fine Arts in Boston, the Virginia Museum of Fine Arts in Richmond, and the Greenwich, Connecticut, chapter of the Garden Clubs of America.

The instructions that follow showcase a condensed, one-day version of my weekend-long Being with Flowers workshop. It is my hope that you will be inspired to include the teachings of this book in your own versions of this workshop, to share the beauty of flowers with your communities.

PREPARATION

I begin by creating a sacred space overflowing with the help and magic of the flowers. I like to arrange chairs, pillows, or back jacks in a circle with a simple, low arrangement of flowers and candles in the center of the circle. Sitting together in a circle is a very inclusive way of sharing. Next, I surround the sitting circle with 6 ft (1.8 m) tables filled with abundant vases of flowers, arranged by type, such as a large cylinder with just birds of paradise in it, or a ginger jar-shaped vase filled with delphinium. I do not worry about fussily arranging these flowers, but leave them simply placed in each vessel.

On one of the tables, I create a main altar, similar to the one featured in chapter 2 under "Create a Personal Altar." I love to include books I cherish about flowers or floral arranging, along with some photo albums of my work. In advance, I prepare a bud vase filled with water for each participant and arrange the bud vases in a circle on the altar table.

It is important to have heart-opening instrumental music playing softly in the background. I find that instrumental music only adds to this experience. Music with vocals and words may be distracting to some.

THE WELCOMING

Once the participants are seated, I begin with a heartfelt prayer, or perhaps with poetry that speaks of the flowers and how they touch us. I often read the first two pages of Eckhart Tolle's *A New Earth*, which really speaks to the deep and ancient connection that exists between flowers and the human family.

At this point, it is nice to offer a prayer of thanksgiving and invite those who have come before us—our ancestors—to join. I often ask participants to honor one such person in their lives with the floral work they do during the workshop, and to keep this person in mind as they work. As the facilitator, I give a brief history at this point of my own journey with the flowers. I also like to share a little about a current project or something that I aspire to create.

THE INTRODUCTIONS

I invite each participant to walk around the space I have created, experiencing the flowers, and ask each participant to choose one single flower and place it in one of the bud vases on the altar. When participants return to the circle, they introduce themselves by name and state what reason (if there is a reason!) they chose that particular flower for their vase, and also why they chose to come to the workshop.

This can lead to some very emotional responses, so I make sure to have tissues ready. The tears often just naturally flow for some people in this setting. It is a circle of flower-loving kindred spirits. People have said that it is at these workshops where, for the first time in their lives, they feel validated for the love they have for flowers. This sharing time sets the tone for the next several hours of creating together.

THE LESSON

I have found that I learn best by observing, as do many others, so I teach by actively demonstrating my technique of conscious floral arranging. In this way, I begin with a 6 in (15 cm) bubble bowl vessel, which will become a 360-degree centerpiece. Participants will be creating one like this very soon, so it is nice to show them one as an example. I like to create two different arrangements, one a classic style, and one that is a more modern presentation.

With various types of flowers and other flora, I slowly walk them through the techniques outlined in chapters 5 and 6. I always remind participants of the importance of natural movement and placement within the arrangements.

THE GATHERING

If the workshop is being held near a public park or wild area, it is nice to carve out a portion of workshop time for mindful gathering. I fill a 5 gal (19 L) bucket with just enough water so that the stems we gather will be in water, but not so much as to be too heavy to carry. Since the workshop space is already full of the flowers that will be the focal points of the creations, what we aim to gather will be pieces to accompany and frame those flowers.

"Consider the lilies, how they grow. They neither toil nor spin."

—JESUS CHRIST

Native grasses, vines, berries, and fruit on the stem are all wonderful options, as are pliable branches, ferns, and ivy. Really, whatever is in abundance in the local area is perfect. I seek permission in advance of the workshop from the owner of the property where we may be gathering whenever possible.

Before we head out, we take a moment as a group to just breathe together and ask each participant to keep in mind what they are gathering for, so that they can be mindful in their choices. This is a time to connect with nature and also with the other participants. It is, as one participant said to me, "very natural for females, the natural gatherers of our species."

Upon return, I ask participants to go through what they have gathered. I have them remove the lower leaves so that when the stems are inserted into their creations there are no leaves in the water. When this is done, I give each participant a bud vase and demonstrate a single flower bud vase creation with just one of the items they gathered as an accent, such as a rose with a bit of ivy.

"Flowers are happy things."

—P. G. WODEHOUSE

THE CREATION

At this point in the workshop, I invite participants to stand or sit at their workstations or whatever is most comfortable for them. I ask them to take a moment, all together, to place their hands on their water-filled vessels and give thanks for the gift of water, the gift of life, and the gift of this moment.

Depending on the amount of allotted time, participants create one or two pieces based on the techniques demonstrated earlier in the workshop. I like to have them start with a 6 in (15 cm) bubble bowl centerpiece. They work with the vines, branches, and grasses they have gathered, paired with the cut flowers I have made available to them.

I like to have lively music playing in the background, because I feel that it adds to the joyous and creative environment. I make myself available to the participants by walking around the room to answer any questions they may have and offer suggestions when needed.

THE GIFT

When everyone is finished with his or her creation, we gather back into the circle. Sometimes it is possible to visibly see how much people are becoming attached to their creations. They may be discussing where they will place it in their home.

At this point in the workshop it is time for a break, so I tell a quick story about the gift of giving. The one I share in the last chapter of this book often gets me all teary-eyed. As they leave for lunch, I ask them to take their new creation with them, walk up to a total stranger, and give it away.

I often get some curious reactions at first, but invariably, when we reconvene there will be stories of how this just made someone's day. Often, the simple act of kindness can be a huge gift to the giver as well.

THE CLOSING

After participants return from their break and have shared their stories about giving away their creations, I like to ask them to create another piece, this time in absolute silence. This shift in mood allows them to be with the flowers in a deeper way.

One of my main teachings is to be clear with your language and intention. We work *with* the flowers, we do not *use* them. I gently remind participants of this subtle yet powerful distinction throughout the workshop.

When participants have finished with their creations, they gather back into a circle and I offer a few closing state-ments, then open the class up for verbal comments as we prepare to depart.

tip

At the end of the workshop, the participants bring their flower and bud vases home with them. I ask them to do the Flower Insight meditation outlined earlier in this chapter. It should be done for at least ten minutes as the last thing done before going to sleep that night, and again in the morning when rising. This can help establish a daily practice of flower consciousness.

Creating in Silence

TO BE FULLY PRESENT for the act of creating with flowers, I
have found that the less distraction there is, the more attention
I can give to what is unfolding before me. When we engage in
conversation, much of our attention is diverted to listening to
others and the thought process of responding to them.

I consider being in silence a luxury.
Civilization often has us dancing a
"How are you?" "Fine . . . and you?"
dance. This dance can be jarring to
the spirit, as it sometimes forces us to
be untruthful. Everyone knows there is
not really enough time in brief passing
to see whether the person asking *really*
wants to know, so we often just do the
dance. Whenever you see me, please
just say hello!

Being in silence when you are
in public requires that you wear a
sign around your neck that states IN
SILENCE in big, bold letters. I prefer
the term IN LOVING SILENCE. Doing
this will startle or even amuse some
people, but most often they will read
it and apologize for talking to you, not
knowing that it is okay for them to talk
to you—it's just not okay for you to talk

to them. If you need to go out in public
while in silence, do wear the sign. It will
help others, even those closest to you,
remember that for this allotted time you
are not going to speak. You may also
want to have a small notepad handy if
you must communicate with others. Do
so only when absolutely necessary.

To experiment with being in silence
while you create, find some time when
you can be in a space alone. Turn off
your phone, the radio, the television,
and anything else that might make
noise. If you have the luxury of complete alone time to do this, you are truly
blessed. I find it helpful to have the
flowers prepared ahead of time. Make
sure there are no leaves that will be in
the water of your creation, and always
give each flower a fresh cut on the stem
as you work.

Now silently check in with your senses. Close your eyes: What do you hear? Breathe deeply: What do you smell? Place your hands together and rub them gently. Our hands should be honored, as they will perform the good work. After ten deep, mindful breaths, open your eyes. If you feel ready, begin to create. And remember to enjoy it!

NOBLE SILENCE

Some traditions observe a deep silence after the evening gathering until after breakfast the next day. It is said to be very healing. The following words can be found on a sign located in Plum Village, Thich Nhat Hanh's home in France: "We allow silence and the calmness we can find there to permeate our flesh and bones."

Letting Go

Life is a series of moment-by-moment events. We have been told by many wise teachers that the more present we are in these moments, the richer life becomes. We can be called to be fully present in a moment by laughter and also by grief. Flowers provide a beautiful, heart-centering way to be fully in the moment.

When I present a flower offering, I am sometimes asked, "How long will it last?" This question removes one from the present. Concern over some future time when the flowers will transform takes one out of the moment. Perhaps the question they intend is more along the lines of "How long can I depend on these flowers looking just like they do at this moment?"

When a flower is in your presence, it is there for you, right then. What really matters is how much you enjoy the flowers in each state of their transformation. Flowers are a beautiful reminder of the temporal nature of our own selves—a time-lapsed version of our own lives, if you will.

MEDITATION:

Give It Away

THE GIVE IT AWAY MEDITATION will help you embrace the gift of giving in a deeper way. It will highlight for you the concept of nonattachment. Giving away something that we cherish is a wonderful way to experience letting go.

When you have completed an arrangement or handheld bouquet that you would love to keep, that might be the right arrangement for this meditation.

Find a place where you can be relatively unnoticed. I like to rise early to do this. Simply place the flower offering in your selected spot and walk away. Give it away, and receive the joy that the gift of giving brings.

I am able to do this in my rural, pictur-esque neighborhood with relative ease. I have done something similar on a grander scale, with 10 ft (3 m) sunflow-ers placed in moss-covered redwood tree stumps.

It is fun to see people's faces light up, sometimes with confused expres-sions, when they drive by a sight like that. When making a public offering, I like to offer this prayer: "May all who look upon the sight of these flowers and other flora be lifted into their hearts."

"Stop wasting time. You have a limited amount of time to do the good that you have come to do."

—OPRAH WINFREY

The Temporal Nature of Flowers

WE ALL HAVE different ways of looking at what we call death. I think you never really know how you feel about it until it hits close to home. I was with a friend when I got the news that my mother had died. My friend said, "I am here for you. Just release whatever you are feeling. I got you." I remember taking a deep breath and waiting for the feelings to arise. What came up, for me, was this great feeling of wonder and calm. It was not sadness; it was this sense of connecting with the mystery of death in a way I never had before.

I was prepared for the inevitability of her death, because one of my sisters had told me she was in the hospital with severe health issues. Maybe this foreknowledge played into how I took the news. Yet each time death has come close like this, I have felt the same. The feeling is one of wonder. It is also a deep reminder to do what I have come here to do in my life.

I did not really know the depth of love I felt for my mother or father until they were gone. I did not know they would never *really* be gone until they left their earthly bodies. When we really love another, it does not take touch or their physical presence to take us to the connective place or conjure the feelings that we call love.

"Wilting flowers do not cause suffering. It is the unrealistic desire that flowers not wilt that causes suffering."

—THICH NHAT HANH

Do you love flowers? Those of us who love flowers are bound together by the way they lift us up. We are kindred spirits because of this. We know that all who take in the glory they have come to give us can be lifted higher into our humanity. This is why we reach out with flowers when a friend's loved one passes. This is why we lay flowers down at the site of loss and destruction. Even angry men in riot gear cannot stamp out the glorious beauty that is offered by a single flower.

Like real love, the sacred gift that flowers give us lives on continuously. It lives on every time a mother, out walking with her little ones in strollers, points and says, "Pretty flowers." It lives on every time you share your love of flowers with others.

The temporal nature of flowers can remind us not to take this breath for granted. Inhaling gardenias, garden roses, plumeria, fragrant lilies, or a host of other flowers can conjure for us what some would call heaven on Earth. Earth, this beautiful blue planet, the only home we know, gifts us every day with life-giving water, soul-stirring sunsets, cool breezes on hot days, and the glory of the garden—*flowers*!

WABI SABI

The Japanese have a spiritual practice that is known as *wabi sabi*. It is the acceptance of things that are transient or imperfect. It is the daily loving of what IS, the honoring of the beauty that is found in all things, whether broken or pristine.

The Gift of Giving

WORKING WITH FLOWERS is first and foremost a gracious gift to yourself. Carving time into your busy schedule to be with the flowers in a creative manner will enhance your life in ways that you can only experience by doing so. Be aware of this sweet gift you are giving yourself during each step of your journey with the flowers. This can help you savor the gift of giving all the more.

Arrange the curly willow inside the vessel. Position the privet leaves around the mouth of the vessel. Garland the ivy around the base of the bowl.

Place pink waxflowers and privet berries to help establish the space that is to be filled.

MATERIALS

Curly willow

6" (15 cm) bubble bowl

Privet berries and leaves

Variegated small-leaved English ivy

Half a bunch of pink waxflowers

One five-stem bunch of daffodils

One ten-stem bunch of alstroemeria

Three blush pink mini calla lilies

Ferns

Native grasses

Add daffodils, alstroemeria, and callas in a way that honors each flower. Remember, you are giving them a new home.

Add ferns and native grasses to complete the offering. This arrangement was offered as part of the Give It Away meditation earlier in this chapter.

Letting Go

SOMETIMES, IN WINTER, I stand under towering deciduous trees and look up at their grand sculpture. These trees provide for us a meaningful lesson in letting go. In autumn, when the time is right, an internal ancient knowledge helps them understand that letting go of their leaves makes room for new beginnings. These leaves will plant seeds of sustenance and energy for regrowth. This release is effortless—it involves simply letting go.

The first time I was hired to create a piece for a public space was an auspicious event. It was for an upscale women's clothing boutique in Aptos, California. It was summer and I worked with 5 ft (1.5 m)-tall sunflowers that I purchased at our farmers' market in Santa Cruz. These sunflowers were paired with robust blue delphinium. The tall cylinder vase was garlanded with large, vibrant, leafy English ivy. There were tiny green apples cascading around the mouth of the vessel. I also added native summer grasses—weeds to some, but beautiful to me.

When I placed the piece, I sat there for a moment and offered the following words silently to the universe: *Please let at least one person deeply see this arrangement. Let it touch them in a way that they are lifted higher into their humanity. If they see beauty, let that beauty remind them of the beauty that is inside them. Let them pass that beauty on.*

Four days later, I received a call from a very kind lady with an open invitation to gather flowers from her garden. She said, "I wish I could grow all the flowers you create with. Please come to my garden anytime and help yourself." We arranged to meet the next day. When I arrived, she greeted me with a gentle hug, and said, "Go right out. I will join you shortly." I walked out to what still remains—after twenty years—the most lush and abundant English country garden I have ever encountered.

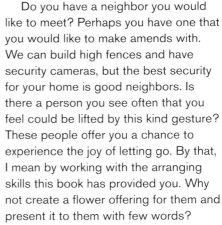

I was in tears almost immediately—just overwhelmed by this answer to the silent prayer I had offered. Even as I write this, tears of thanksgiving and joy well up in my eyes. An answer like this to my silent prayer was beyond anything I had imagined. This kind lady was so moved by the arrangement that she invited a total stranger to her home to share in the abundance of this sacred garden.

This is the true heart of letting go. It is the joyful relinquishing of something we hold dear, just because we can. In my journey with the flowers, I am given the joy and honor of connecting with people in the context of sharing beauty with them. The act of letting go is one of the aspects of this work that I hold most dear. Without expectation, like the deciduous tree in autumn, it requires simply letting go.

Do you have a neighbor you would like to meet? Perhaps you have one that you would like to make amends with. We can build high fences and have security cameras, but the best security for your home is good neighbors. Is there a person you see often that you feel could be lifted by this kind gesture? These people offer you a chance to experience the joy of letting go. By that, I mean by working with the arranging skills this book has provided you. Why not create a flower offering for them and present it to them with few words?

I create floral arrangements for a wide variety of events. When some events are over, there are many flowers that get left behind. I always try to figure out a way to share this bounty with others. One of my favorite ways to do this is to place single blooms in water tubes, go out into the street, and just pass them out to whoever happens by.

I once did this in New York City after an event at which Zen Master Thich Nhat Hanh spoke. This was so fitting, because he often punctuates his teaching with examples of how flowers can be our teachers. "The entire cosmos exists in the sunflower. You can see this if you look deeply into its smiling face," he says. "The clouds are in a sunflower, because clouds make water and without water there would be no sunflower."

When this particular event was over, I gathered close to one hundred flowers and went out to share this bounty on the streets near Broadway and Times Square. I was met with many joyful reactions, as well as some curious and even disgruntled (at first) facial expressions. The frowns turned upside down when I simply reached out to hand passersby a flower.

I try not to talk much when I do this—just smiling and handing someone a flower speaks volumes. However, one person really stood out on this particular day. She was an elderly Asian lady with long pigtails and she was wearing a crisp, impeccably ironed maid's uniform. I reached out to hand her a flower and she just hurried past me. I followed her and said, "This is for you."

She started crying almost immediately. "You don't understand. I love flowers so very much, but I cannot afford this, so please just go away!"

I told her the flower was of no cost. "It is free and it is for you."

Then she began almost convulsing and sat down on a bench. I gave her a bottle of water as I had an extra and then got up to walk away. She said, "You know, young man, no one has ever done something like this for me. You are so kind. How did you know that flowers are my favorite part of life?"

I told her, "I do not know, but the flowers do," and then smiled and walked away. I looked back and she was just sitting there, smelling the fragrant freesia I had shared with her, tears still streaming down her face. When our tears fall, it is a way that we heal ourselves.

Since I often have leftover flowers after events, when I stay at hotels and tip the maid at checkout, I like to leave a small floral offering as well. I believe it is important to honor those who often go unseen. Of the many wise things Maya Angelou shared with us, my favorite is: "If you learn, teach . . . If you get, give."

The temporal nature of the flower itself has much to teach us. It helps us learn to appreciate the beauty in each moment, to be present, and then to release the moment, or the flower, once its time has passed. A beautiful arrangement can transform greatly within a week. Our awareness of the flower's life cycle can be transferred into an awareness of our own temporal nature, a reminder to live life in the present and appreciate the beauty that is, before it is gone.

Acknowledgments

I give a deep bow of thanks to the following people:

My grandparents, Alvis and Luvie White, Dollie Mae Hall, and John Oscar Ward.

All of my siblings—Ann, Denise, Oscar, Louis, Dee Dee, Michelle, and Michael, as well as my brothers-in-law Bob and Galen, my nephews A.J., Sam, Silas, Charles Agent, and Little Oscar, and my niece Chelsea.

This book would not have been written without the enthusiasm, syntax, and good humor of Brooke St. George, my writer-editor in this endeavor. Brooke is a deeply gifted writer with several of her own projects in the works. Most of the images in this book were captured by John Felix at the California home of Angela Miller. Thank you also to Veda Flanagan for all of the technical support.

Thank you to Jonathan Simcosky for reaching out to me and establishing the avenue for the creation of this book. Thank you also to Marissa Giambrone for her artistic vision, Cara Connors, and the rest of the team at Quarto for making this book possible.

A very special thanks to my first and main floral mentor, the late Wilbur G. Davis, master florist, and to my other floral mentors, Sandra Parks and Rebecca Cole.

I offer my deep thanks to the following people who have assisted me in various and substantial ways over the years: Joel Devalcourt, Kai Lillie, Marcel Menard, Jon Morrison Cavanaugh and the Cavanaugh Color Family, William Atwell, Sebastian Stanton-Clarke, Hudson Soules, Jeroch Carlson, Jerod Black, Ivette Rosado, Gary Wayne Carter, Ira Ellis Schwartz, Jacob Purcy, and Konrad Van Spall.

During my twelve-year tenure at Omega Institute, I was graciously assisted at various times by the following people: Josiah Bump, Jacob Williamson, Alex Grace, Christian Monsen, Allen Edwards, Cleary, Adam Kistner, Trevor Batchelder, Michael Landers Barry, Shaun Berhoe, and William Addison. Thank you also to Pam Vitarious, the Omega gardener.

A big thank-you to the following people who were so helpful to me in Santa Cruz: Sean and George, Annie Morhauser of Annie Glass, Linda Pope of Pope Gallery, David Mills and Stephanie Lynn-Mills, John and Betty Devalcourt, Dave and Nancy Cavanaugh, Karl Schneider and Vanessa Lillie, Beverly Bacack, Geraldine Drago, Barbara Horscraft, the Santa Cruz Art Center, and the Santa Cruz Symphony Orchestra.

Special thanks to Omega Institute, Mount Madonna Center, Kripalu Center for Yoga and Health, Misti and George at George's Geodes and Gems, and my local community garden. I would like to thank my dance teachers Denise Donlon, Bill Goodson, Carol Connors, and Sojourner Trouissant.

The following notable people have been most instrumental along my journey with the flowers. I thank you all deeply for encouraging me in your own special way. Thank you all so very much for sharing your support, wisdom, guidance, and encouragement: His Holiness the Dalai Lama, Thich Nhat Hanh, H.H. Pujya Swami Chidanand Saraswatiji, Eckhart Tolle, Maya Angelou, Ram Dass, Adyashanti, Deepak Chopra, Pema Chödrön, Alice Walker, the late Babatunde Olatunji, the late Odetta, Don Miguel Ruiz, Jane Fonda, Eve Ensler, The Thirteen Indigenous Grandmothers, Jane Goodall, Joan Halifax, Patrick Horvath, Alex and Allyson Grey, Eli Morgan,

Further Collective, Chris Bohlin, Chris Dyer, Robert Venosa and Martina Hoffmann, Gurmukh and Gurushabd Khalsa, Michael Franti and Sara Agah Franti, Spearhead, Catherine Enny, Julia Butterfly Hill, Iyanla Vanzant, Sam Keen, Robert and Nena Thurman, Jack Kornfield, John Perkins, Uma Thurman, Ani DiFranco, Linda Goldstein, Bobby McFerrin, Kira Lillie, LeAnna Cargman, Cathline Marshall, Saul Williams, Amy Goodman, Ben Harper, Freedom Child, Chrissie Hynde, Rising Appalachia, Brett Dennen, Sarah Siskind and Travis Book, Bette Midler, Zap Mama, Philip Glass, Alanis Morissette, FKA Twigs, Ethan Hawke, Diane Keaton, the late Melissa Mathison Ford, Anna Sui, Kate Pierson, Keith Strickland, Depeche Mode, Bonnie Raitt, Kerry Washington, Rosie O'Donnell, Gayle King, Diane von Furstenberg, Jessye Norman, Sweet Honey in the Rock, Mary McFadden, Jennifer Hudson, John Perkins, Eric Spire, Sound Tribe Sector 9, Desert Dwellers, Tipper, Bluetech, Random Rab, OTT, Bassnector, Flying Lotus, Kalya Scintilla and Eve Olution, Deva Premal and Miten, Snatam Kaur, Emancipator, Sally Field, Cindra Ladd, Belinda Carlisle, Isabel Allende, Brian Wingate, and Nakona MacDonald.

I thank you for sharing your sacred resource of time to explore the pages of this book.

I am in constant thanks to and praise of our beautiful blue planet Earth, the only home we know, for pouring forth the magic and glory of FLOWERS: Fantastic Love Offerings Welcoming Everyone Revealing Souls.

About the Author

Visionary floral sculptor Anthony Ward is an artist and businessman living in northern California. He travels the world sharing his deep love of flowers by creating for weddings, teaching workshops, and creating public and private altars and "prayerformances" at transformational festivals. He and Christopher Issa are currently producing the feature-length documentary *Dancing with the FLOWERS*. Anthony can be found online at www.beingwithflowers.com, on Facebook and Instagram at Anthony Flowers Ward, and on Twitter *@floralsculptor*. His team also operates the Facebook pages Being with Flowers, Live Visionary Floral Art, and Flower Buddha.

Index

Also Available

Brave Intuitive Painting
978-1-59253-768-6

Creative Revolution
978-1-63159-259-1

Cloud Sketching
978-1-63159-095-5

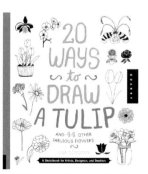

20 Ways to Draw a Tulip
978-1-59253-886-7